£3.50

LOCOMOTIVE PROFILE

Type 5 Freight Diesels

David N. Clough

LONDON
IAN ALLAN LTD

First published 1990

ISBN 0 7110 1875 8

Published by Ian Allan Ltd, Shepperton, Surrey; and printed by Ian Allan Printing Ltd at their works at Coombelands in Runnymede, England

Front cover:
The impressive bulk of Class 56 No 56081 at Birkenhead North Open Day on 6 April 1986.
C. Wellum

Back cover:
Class 58 No 58002 powers a southbound MGR coal train through Oxford station on 22 March 1989. *Paul Mills*

This page:
Class 58 No 58012 passes Ironville with a northbound MGR on 9 August 1985. *L. A. Nixon*

Previous page:
Class 58 No 58028 is seen at Acton Wells Junction with the 6Z69 Northfleet-Toton MGR empties on 29 October 1988.
Michael J. Collins

Contents

Introduction

Thirty years have now elapsed since the first products of the 1955 Modernisation Plan entered service, and the fourth generation of diesels to run on BR is currently being evolved. During the years in between a variety of concepts and specifications have served to shape the Railway's fleet and the objective of this book is to examine how the current Type 5 freight prime movers have evolved. A number of factors have influenced the process: politics, personalities and available technology. Most enthusiasts do not appreciate these matters. Somewhat naturally, BR staff are reluctant to voice opinions which may not square with that of senior management and the true story only emerges several years on, after key figures have departed or policy changes are introduced arising from admitted weakness in previous attitudes and methods.

The shaping and reshaping of BR's requirements for large freight locomotives contains all the elements mentioned above. Whilst undoubtedly the full story has not been unearthed, and some aspects still remain *sub judice* the book will have achieved something if a better understanding of the position is possessed by the reader when he has finished it. Many books seem reluctant to tell the truth if it is critical; indeed some actually present a misleading picture, leaving the reader with the impression that everything is fine when, in reality, it is not. Here there will be no deliberate intention to disguise reality. In doing so, though, the background to a problem must be understood. Notable in this respect is the ever-increasing financial stringency under which BR operates. This means, for example, spare part stockholdings may be unable to meet a peak demand for a component, causing locomotives to stand waiting under repair. Staff attitude and morale is also vital, as was seen as a result of the London Midland Region's Lococare drive of 1986/87. Interest in the job and a sense of purpose yield better results, but when maintenance staff have been working on the same machines for over 20 years, motivation can be a problem.

The foregoing would suggest that what is to come will be a catalogue of bad news but this is not the case. The fact that Britain has a locomotive industry capable of winning overseas business shows that its products must be both capable and competitive. It must be said that their design work has, largely, been directed towards meeting the needs of the home market and this is where there is interface between engineering expertise and politics and personalities. Further, the Americans readily admit that the standard of training and expertise possessed by BR's maintenance staff is generally far superior to that found in their country, let alone some of the less well-developed nations of the world. By way of illustration, at the time this book was being written, Class 58 was achieving 86% availability, an excellent figure in terms of the way the figure is calculated.

Having provided the background to the story, it is now worth outlining how it will be told. Firstly, the origins of the large diesel locomotive on BR will be examined to see the factors influencing the first and second generation Type 4s. Following this, the two prototypes, Kestrel and No 47601, will be discussed to place them in the scheme of things. Having then reached the stage of the emergence of the third generation machines, the Type 5 freight designs of Classes 56 and 58, each will be examined in some detail, both technically and operationally. Then the influence of Class 59 will lead the way towards the final chapter which considers future plans.

Many people have contributed to the research for this book. Special mention must go to my good friends Mike Hunt (who has been a great help in the provision of material and checking the text), Chris Holland and David Rapson (for research material) and Peter Boyce (for proof reading). The publicity departments of Brush Electrical Machines Ltd and Ruston Diesels Ltd have also been of assistance. Acknowledgement is also made in respect of material obtained from the proceedings of the Institution of Mechanical Engineers and the magazine of the Railway Correspondence & Travel Society. This book has been written by a layman who has no engineering training and it is, therefore, hoped that fellow laymen and enthusiasts will be able to enjoy the text, even though the subject matter is, at times, a little complicated.

CHAPTER 1

Historical Background

Even though the Type 5s currently found on BR come from different stables, being of both British and American origin, the features found in them have evolved in a similar way. It will therefore be useful to follow this evolutionary process, using British main line diesel traction as the example, to show why the present classes are the way that they are.

The two LMS-commissioned prototypes, Nos 10000/1, built at Derby in 1947/48, provided a basic design formula which was to hold good for many years. A cab, mounted at each end, has remained standard practice, whilst the use of a bogie with all axles driven, to give maximum available adhesion, has also been a cornerstone, save for a short interlude to be described in a moment. Available technology limited the diesel engine output to 1,600bhp in 1947, but the use of only one diesel engine in the bodyshell has again been accepted as best practice, due to the lower maintenance cost of a single large unit rather than two small ones. For British application, electric transmission has remained the usual method of converting and controlling the diesel engine output into useful tractive capability.

The biggest restriction which the first two prototypes faced was their axle loading. A weight of more than 127 tons spread over six axles, did not permit a wide route availability. The problem was the method of construction used, with a substantial underframe giving rise to a high total weight. As constructional techniques had not advanced when the SR-commissioned prototypes, Nos 10201-3, were built, the Chief Mechanical Engineer, O. V. S. Bulleid, was obliged to spread the weight over eight axles and so the Ashford drawing office designed a 1-Co bogie with the leading axle on each bogie being unpowered. This brought the axle loading down from over 22 tons (in the case of Nos 10000/1) to 18 tons (for Nos 10201-3). The last of the trio, No 10203, was delayed so that the English

Electric diesel engine, used in all these prototypes, could be fitted in its uprated form, delivering 2,000bhp; this represented a 25% increase since its first use in No 10000.

In 1955 the British Transport Commission (BTC), the predecessor to the British Railways Board (BRB), announced its Modernisation Plan. Three large diesel designs were envisaged. One was to be a diesel-hydraulic, the other two, though, were to be similar to No 10203. Of the latter, one was to come from the English Electric Company (EE) and one was to be designed by Derby works. Both were twin cab, single power unit diesel electrics, employing the Bulleid 1-Co bogie to spread their bulk of more than 130 tons to allow them fairly wide route availability. A pilot batch of 10 of each was ordered, the EE locomotives becoming D200-9 (later Class 40) and the Derby products D1-10, the 'Peaks' (later Class 44).

With the abandonment of the original plan for evaluation of the various Pilot Scheme designs, as the BTC considered rapid dieselisation was a better solution to some of the problems then facing the railways, the decision was taken to multiply the designs already in traffic. This brought about the construction of the B-B Class 42 and 43 diesel-hydraulics, as successors to the D600 prototypes and further batches of EE Class 40s and Derby 'Peaks'. Although the Sulzer diesel fitted to the new 'Peaks', later Classes 45 and 46, had been uprated slightly from 2,300bhp to 2,500bhp, they were still very heavy for the power available and compared most unfavourably with the Class 42 and 43 'Warships'; the respective power-to-weight ratios were 18.5hp and 20.2hp per ton whilst the EE D200s offered only 15hp per ton of locomotive weight. Faced with such an advantage it might have been natural for the BTC to have opted outright for a diesel-hydraulic configuration, but here personalities creep in. The only supporter of the hydraulic option was the WR; the BTC's senior engineering management being wedded to the concept of a medium-speed diesel powering an electric generator.

Having ordered nearly 400 diesel-electrics with 1-Co wheel arrangement, by the dawning of the 1960s, BR realised that a better power-to-weight ratio would be needed in the large diesels, to give the opportunity for faster scheduling for passenger and freight trains. From this emerged the second generation of Type 4 diesels. Several interested manufacturers produced prototypes for evaluation. This brought forth the Brush *Falcon*, which used two high-speed diesels to give 2,800bhp, the Birmingham Railway Carriage & Wagon Co (BRCW) *Lion*, using an uprated version of the Sulzer engine found in the 'Peaks' and now delivering 2,750bhp and the EE offering of DP2, which used an uprated Class 40 diesel to deliver 2,700bhp. All three designs used electric transmission and weighed around 105 to 115 tons. The power-to-weight ratio had now risen to 24bhp per ton, comparable with the new large diesel-hydraulic design, the 'Western', which provided 2,760bhp for a total weight of around 110 tons.

The lower weight of the diesel-electrics had come about partly by the adoption of techniques used in aircraft construction, whereby a stressed-skin superstructure acts as a load-bearing unit so that the heavyweight underframe, used hitherto, could be dispensed with. Equally, technological advancement allowed a diesel engine capable of delivering nearly double the output it could in 1947, with constructional methods refined to reduce the overall mass so that a 19½-ton axle load could be offered when the locomotive was mounted on Co-Co bogies, thereby allowing all available weight to be used for adhesion. The three second-generation prototypes had little bearing on the selection of the standard large Type 4 for the 1960s as, again politics and personalities intervened. The BTC Chief Mechanical & Electrical Engineer considered the Sulzer 2,750bhp unit was the only 'right and proper' one of the contenders, whilst regional lobbying saw Brush awarded the initial order for 20 locomotives, Nos D1500-19, the company winning subsequent re-orders until over 500 had been built.

The D1500 design, Class 47 as it was later to become, has proved to be a success, after the early troubles with the Sulzer engine had been overcome. Success is judged here in terms of rates of availability and reliability generally better than the other BR large Type 4s and running costs at least as good, often better. These

Below left:
The English Electric Co was a pioneer of diesel traction in Britain. Its collaboration with the LMS led to the standard diesel shunter, later Class 08. Collaboration with the LMS also gave rise to two main line locomotives which were equally to have a significant bearing on the shape of the BR fleet. In this picture, taken at Euston prior to rebuilding, the second of the LMSR-inspired products, No 10001, is seen alongside another EE prototype, *Deltic*.
GEC Traction

Left:
The Southern Railway also commenced work on a main line diesel design in conjunction with EE. Three examples were built, numbered 10201-3, an interesting feature being the 1-Co bogie (clearly visible here) which was used under the first generation BR Type 4s. *GEC Traction*

Right:
The English Electric Co Type 4 (later Class 40) was one of two diesel-electric designs of 2,000bhp or more ordered by the British Transport Commission in 1955 as part of its Modernisation Plan. It proved to be a very reliable and quite versatile design, covering just about every sort of job on the Railway. A drawback, though, was its limited power, which later relegated it to second rank express passenger work. Summer Saturday traffic across the Pennines provided Class 40 with some Class 1 work until the early 1980s. On 14 July 1981 an unidentified locomotive prepares to enter Standedge Tunnel at Marsden with the 09.25 Newcastle to Blackpool North, whilst a Class 47 emerges at the head of the 09.00 Llandudno-York.
David N. Clough

Left:
When BR came to order its second generation standard mixed traffic Type 4 the Brush/Sulzer offering was chosen. Later to become Class 47, it was used on the ER on MGR coal movements from their inception in the mid-1960s. Train formations proved beyond the continuous rating capacity of the main generator, bringing failures and a consequent reduction to only 30 HAA vehicles. It was this limitation which, in part, brought the need for a prime mover better able to cope with heavy freight. Spring sunshine lights up Knottingley-based No 47373 as it threads the maze of track to the south of Doncaster with an empty rake of MGRs; the date is 26 March 1976.
L. A. Nixon

criteria, however, have certain limitations. All the designs discussed so far were specified as mixed traffic. This meant configuring a performance curve which would make them suitable for express passenger work at 90mph and yet also be able to haul heavy freight; inevitably both objectives were compromised to some extent. Class 47 was no exception. In derated form, following the engine cracking problems referred to above, the Class 47s could only deliver full power up to 75mph, a relatively low figure by comparison with the other Type 4s. Further, they had a high continuous rating speed of 27mph, which meant that care was needed when working heavy freight trains not to exceed the short-term ratings of, in particular, the main generator. Use on merry-go-round (MGR) traffic in South Yorkshire in the mid-1960s highlighted this and trains had to be reduced from 34 to 30 HAA wagons following a spate of main generator failures. The class was generally not fitted with sanding gear, a feature omitted from its design due to the fashion of the time on BR, and this imposes limitations on the locomotives' tractive capability. Finally, the use of contactors and relays within the control circuits, components which are (relatively) slow to react to signals from the driver, mean that responsiveness to wheelslip correction is not as good as the electronic-based systems adopted in subsequent designs.

Class 47 was delivered between 1962 and 1967. In 1965 a need was perceived for a further batch of large Type 4s but fatigue cracks were just emerging in the engines fitted to the class. Although EE had bid for the repeat orders which had resulted in the Brush Type 4 being multiplied to over 500 it had been unsuccessful in obtaining an order for these further batches of large Type 4s. This was not due to any failings on the part of its prototype, DP2, which was still performing admirably on the Eastern Region. Having considered the options, BR decided to award the contract for what was to be the final batch of large Type 4 mixed traffic locomotives to EE. Although the latter had expected a specification for 50 DP2s, this proved not to be quite the case. Senior staff within the Chief Mechanical & Electrical Engineer's (CM&EE) department had views on how the new

locomotive should be equipped and in a farsighted decision they specified the use of first generation electronics within the control system.

This decision had its critics and brought problems. Some argued against the 'complexity' which the adoption of electronics brought, but this was nothing more than a Luddite response to changing times. Being the first class on BR to make substantial use of electronics meant that maintenance staff had to undergo retraining and their unfamiliarity hampered the expedition of repairs, whilst the electronics were blamed for every failure, whether justly or not. In the 1980s no-one would seriously consider other than to employ electronic components in locomotive control; in fact the much-admired wheelslip control system in Class 59 could not function without them. Once the decision had been taken on the basic control system for the new EE Type 4, which was to become Class 50, it became possible to utilise its versatility to incorporate sub-systems such as slow speed control and precise limiting of tractive effort under driver operation. The resultant locomotive was accordingly a very highly specified machine, which could outperform any other Type 4 either in express passenger or freight haulage. A further interesting point was that opinions were obviously shifting over the wisdom of having sanding available, for the new fleet included provision for fitting such equipment.

The appearance of D400 in the autumn of 1967 marked the high point of the mixed traffic Type 4 on BR. Final withdrawal of steam the following year, coupled with declining traffic, meant there was no further need for additional diesels and, indeed, it became possible to weed out the less successful types (in terms of running costs and reliability) which, in the Type 4 category, meant the Class 42 and 43 'Warships', followed later by the Class 52 'Westerns'; diesel-electric propulsion had finally won the day. The situation remained thus until events on the world stage brought a need for change. Following the oil crisis in 1972/73 the Central Electricity Generating Board (CEGB) was forced to shift its fuel supply policies in favour of home-produced coal and this, in turn, required more BR locomotives.

CHAPTER 2
HS4000 *Kestrel*

In the early 1960s the need in terms of horsepower perceived by BR for the majority of its diesel-hauled services was that of its new standard Type 4, 2,750bhp. True, the ac electrics on the London-Birmingham-Liverpool/Manchester railway were considerably more powerful, able to apply 3,300hp at the rail, whilst the principal East Coast main line passenger duties were covered by the 22 Type 5 'Deltics' of 3,300bhp. The latter represented something of a blind alley in terms of rail traction. At the time they were ordered they met a need which could not have been fulfilled by any other existing design available to BR. Using two high speed diesel engines, configured into two power unit sets within each locomotive, a higher power was available than a conventional single, medium-speed diesel could develop, so allowing heavier trains to be moved more quickly. In service the 'Deltic' diesels proved costly to maintain, whilst their generators were prone to flashover, this on top of higher initial cost. That the application of the 'Deltic' diesel engine to rail use was not a complete success can be judged by the early demise of the Type 2 'Baby Deltics'. Whilst the 'Deltics', later Class 55, ran millions of miles on the East Coast main line until their final demise in the early 1980s, their overall performance would have been untenable for a standard class.

The 'Deltics' were not unique in world railway terms, for American railroads also operated twin power unit diesel-electrics or even 'master and slave' couplings of two or more units on a permanent basis. Analysis of the costs, capital maintenance and fuel, showed that the cheapest arrangement was a single machine, fitted with a single power unit. (A power unit is the diesel engine and generator coupled to it.)

It was fortunate that BR did not want more installed power, for it would have been difficult for the technology of the time to supply this unless two or more power units were used. The stumbling block was the capacity of the

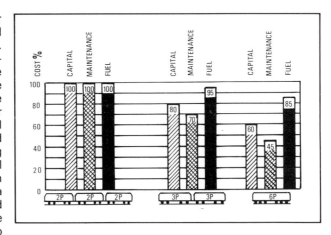

Figure 1: A chart comparing the capital, maintenance and fuel costs of multiple-unit and single-unit high power units

main generator. Whilst series wound dc traction motors offer a better low-speed torque characteristic than ac motors, the dc generators which supply power to the motors were right on the limit in coping with 2,750hp due to commutation problems. This difficulty was overcome with ac power generation but the rectifiers produced in the early 1960s were not very reliable, as was found with the ac electrics. Brush had developed a brushless alternator and rectifier set for industrial applications and the advances in electronic engineering assisted in improving the rectifiers. The company had, since 1965, been carrying out development work towards applying this technology for railway locomotives in its prototype *Hawk*, which served as a mobile laboratory. By virtue of this service use in *Hawk*, one of the features of the Brush ac power generation equipment, the incorporation of a short-circuit device, had been tried out. This device, which acted as a switch on the main alternator winding, diverted fault current away from the traction motors and so offered protection from flashovers.

Above:
The EE Co 'Deltics' were the first Type 5s to operate on BR. Ordered for the haulage of the principal East Coast expresses, they were geared accordingly and were not ideal for heavy freight. In service, they proved to be less reliable and more costly than the production Type 4 designs and were not considered as a basis when BR sought a dedicated freight Type 5. In their final years the class put in some very fast running on the King's Cross-Hull trains. No 55021 passes Yaxley on 19 September 1981 with the 09.36 up service. *C. R. Holland*

BR's views on its power needs did not remain fixed for long, as by 1965 it perceived that fending off road and air competition would involve higher speeds and, possibly, heavier loads. The BRB therefore considered a number of options, one of which was a 4,000bhp 'Deltic'. A meeting with Brush in July of that year, however, made it clear that the ideal solution was a single-engined locomotive. As a result of this, Brush, together with its parent company, Hawker Siddeley, commenced work on a project to fulfil BR's needs and this turned into the prototype *Kestrel*.

The Swiss Sulzer company had produced a 16-cylinder version of its LVA24 diesel which had completed Union Internationale des Chemins de fer (UIC) testing at a 4,000 metric horsepower (3,946bhp) rating, operating at 1,100rpm. Accordingly this was selected to power the prototype; the engine was built in France. Its installation produced the world's most powerful single-diesel-unit locomotive. Coupled to it was a Brush BL120-50 ac generator and rectifier set, rated at 2,520kW, at 1,100rpm. A Brush BL63-38 combined auxiliary and train heat generator was driven through a step-up gearbox at 2½ times engine speed through a gearbox. It gave a maximum output of 530kVa at 1,100rpm engine speed and also incorporated an ac exciter to avoid the need for slip-rings and brushes. Power from the main alternator, following rectification, was fed to six Brush TM73-68 Mk 4 traction motors, which were a development of those used in the Brush-equipped Class 46. As such, the rating of the motors had increased from 340hp to 531hp, the continuous rating for use in *Kestrel* being 830A, 522V at 681rpm, the gear ratio being 19:60. Arrangement of the motors was in all-parallel. In addition to the usual driver's antislip brake, a rapid-acting power reduction system was incorporated to prevent wheelslip, which could cut power immediately slipping was detected. To demonstrate the way the pendulum was swinging, after a break with the Class 47s, sanding gear was fitted.

The six traction motors were mounted on two three-axle bogies to give a Co-Co wheel arrangement. Bogie design was based on the Commonwealth bogie used previously by Brush in its Type 2 and Type 4 fleets but incorporated a hydraulic parking brake. Gearing was for mixed traffic duties. This offered full power at about 18mph, a continuous rating speed of 27.5mph, a continuous top speed of 110mph, service maximum of 125mph and design limit of 130mph. With two stages of traction motor field weakening full power was available up to 100mph, yet there was plenty of torque at low speed for freight duties. Maximum tractive effort was given as 70,000lb and the continuous rating figure as 41,200lb.

Design work was in collaboration with BR and this is perhaps reflected in parallel work then in progress between EE and BR on the Class 50 project. Thus an electronic control system was specified, as also was dynamic braking. Primary air filtration made use of inertia filters, though in the case of *Kestrel* these were more in keeping with American practice by being roof-mounted pendant types. The 'free float' driver's vigilance device was also found in Class 50.

Internally the power unit was situated amidships. At No 1 end was the main cooler group and dynamic brake equipment. At No 2 end were the inertia filters, the cooler group for the intercoolers and the main control cubicle. Care was exercised at the design stage to make components which required regular servicing to be easily accessible, with other items being designed to be as maintenance-free as possible. It was estimated this

would save one-third of the time taken to maintain the smaller Brush Type 4. Cab layout and instrumentation was well planned and user-friendly. As with the engine room (by virtue of the pressurising fan used with the inertia filters) the cabs were slightly pressurised and this helped keep out draughts. Fully adjustable driver's seats, which were well padded, were installed. Train crews were pleased with the environment.

Body construction was of the stressed skin type and was basically similar to the Brush Type 4. Indeed, the length over buffers, at 66ft 6in, was only 3ft longer than the Type 4, a further demonstration of how advancing technology allowed 40% more power to be accommodated into virtually the same size of body. Nose ends were semi-streamlined and wrap-round Triplex windscreens were fitted. A two-tone livery of yellow and chocolate brown was adopted and the number HS4000 carried. Construction was at the Brush Falcon works at Loughborough. A design weight of 126 tons was aimed for, giving a 21-ton axleload.

Kestrel went to Derby works on 20 January 1968 for weighing and this revealed a significant problem; at 133 tons it was rather heavier than planned, the excess being due to the difficulty in gauging things with a prototype. On 29 January a formal handing-over cer-

emony took place at Marylebone, with the chairmen of Hawker Siddeley, Brush and the BRB being present. During the spring test running was carried out between Crewe and Carlisle, including the haulage of a 650-ton train over Shap at 46mph. During the tests, when No 1 end was leading, excessive engine room temperatures were recorded, whilst exhaust was drawn into the locomotive; this was remedied by fitting baffles in the engine room to improve air flow. Whilst it had been intended to put *Kestrel* into passenger service, by virtue of it having axle-hung traction motors and an axle loading of over 22 tons this was not possible. Following the tests associated with the track stresses imposed by nose-suspended traction motors on ac electrics, the Civil Engineer decreed a maximum axle load of 20 tons for 100mph running, so clearly *Kestrel* was a non-starter.

Accordingly it was allocated to Tinsley depot on 14 May, sub-shedded at Shirebrook, and began work the following day on coal traffic between Mansfield and Whitemoor, making two return trips daily on a five days a week basis. Trailing loads were between 1,450 tons and 1,600 tons, the same as for a Brush Type 4 at the time, due to problems accommodating longer trains in loops and sidings. Daily mileage was about 360 and, with speed limited by virtue of the wagons to 35mph, the

Above left:
Kestrel's distinctive profile is captured in this view taken at Princes Risborough on 29 January 1968 prior to making the return trip to Marylebone. *Euslin Bruce*

Above:
The special train of invited guests departs from Princes Risborough, 29 January 1968.
Euslin Bruce

**Figure 2: HS4000 *Kestrel*
General Arrangement**

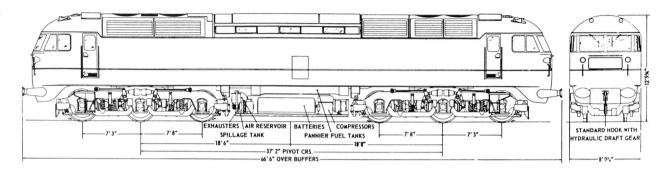

7' 3"   7' 8"

EXHAUSTERS   AIR RESERVOIR
SPILLAGE TANK   BATTERIES   COMPRESSORS
PANNIER FUEL TANKS   7' 8"   7' 3"

18' 6"   18' 8"

37' 2" PIVOT CRS.

66' 6" OVER BUFFERS

STANDARD HOOK WITH
HYDRAULIC DRAFT GEAR

12' 9¾"

8' 9½"

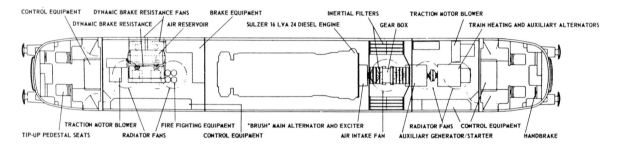

CONTROL EQUIPMENT   DYNAMIC BRAKE RESISTANCE FANS   BRAKE EQUIPMENT   INERTIAL FILTERS   TRACTION MOTOR BLOWER
DYNAMIC BRAKE RESISTANCE   AIR RESERVOIR   SULZER 16 LVA 24 DIESEL ENGINE   GEAR BOX   TRAIN HEATING AND AUXILIARY ALTERNATORS

TRACTION MOTOR BLOWER   FIRE FIGHTING EQUIPMENT   "BRUSH" MAIN ALTERNATOR AND EXCITER   RADIATOR FANS   CONTROL EQUIPMENT
TIP-UP PEDESTAL SEATS   RADIATOR FANS   CONTROL EQUIPMENT   AIR INTAKE FAN   AUXILIARY GENERATOR/STARTER   HANDBRAKE

capabilities of so powerful a machine were not extended. During one daily cycle, a total of 19hr was spent working, of which only 6min was spent at full power. Under such an easy regime it is hardly surprising that availability of up to 90% was attained.

On 11 August *Kestrel* went to Derby for more tests, this time between Derby, Crewe and Nuneaton. As part of the trailing load ac electric locomotive No E3122 was included to provide additional resistance using its dynamic brake and also to tow the train, with *Kestrel* in the rear, to test the latter's dynamic brake. A tractive effort of 85,900lb was recorded at 10.3mph, significantly above the 66,000lb predicted on the published tractive effort/speed curve. Even so, this only equates to some 2,360hp at rail, well below what one would expect, even at a speed below the full power level of about 18mph.

This low level of power, relative to that installed, was borne out in other runs and in terms of the alternator output of 3,340hp. Allowing about 90% traction motor efficiency, the hp at the rail would be around 3,000, consistent for six traction motors each rated continuously at 515hp each, but this was only 75% of engine output where about 80% would be normal. During the trials a top speed of 102mph was permitted, no doubt with ease, but significantly below the design maximum of 130mph.

It was also during August that a special test run was arranged between Mansfield and Lincoln hauling a load of 2,028 tons, by a fraction, the heaviest ever handled to that date on BR. On a wet rail, the use of three-quarters power resulted in some slipping during a restart on a 1 in 150 incline but the electronic control system coped with this and the train was accelerated to 15mph in 7min. A second restart with one-quarter controller saw no wheelslip. Apparently as a result of these tests, a hundred sets of the Brush electronic wheelslip control system were ordered for fitting to Brush Type 4s.

On 22 November *Kestrel* returned to Shirebrook to resume revenue-earning service after some attention at Falcon works. By the end of 1968 about 26,000 miles had been run, of which 22,000 miles were run in traffic. Matters continued thus, operating coal movements out of Shirebrook, until 2 April 1969 when *Kestrel* returned to Loughborough for the fitting of a pair of Class 47 bogies to reduce overall weight sufficiently for diagramming on 100mph passenger turns. The gear ratio then became 53 : 18. Whilst this exchange reduced the weight of the locomotive to about 125 tons, this was still over the 20-ton axleload limit. Further, in Class 47 the traction motors were rated continuously at 368hp each, 2,208hp in aggregate; now they were having to produce 531hp each, a testimony to the faith put in them. Bearing in mind the troubles which have emerged with these motors when fitted to Class 47s used on protracted high-speed runs, it would have been interesting to see how they would have fared in *Kestrel* under extended service conditions.

Back in traffic by mid-June 1969, crew training on the East Coast main line was needed before taking up a 'Deltic' diagram from mid-October, the first recorded visit to King's Cross seemingly being on 18 October. The workings usually covered were the 07.55 King's Cross-Newcastle and 16.45 return whilst in April 1970 *Kestrel* was noted on the King's Cross-Hull Freightliner. On 2 September HS4000 was observed leaving Vickers works at Barrow, where it had been for engine examination, and the only reliable reports subsequent to this date show it back on its old freight turns out of Shirebrook. O. S. Nock published details of a Glasgow-Crewe run in February 1971 but later cast doubt on the reliability of the information, though the timing would fit in with the visit to Barrow. With no prospect of future repeat orders Brush sold the locomotive to the USSR in 1971 and it was withdrawn from service in March/April (sources differ on the point and being on loan to BR it fell

outside the scope of official lists) for attention at Crewe works to prepare it for use in Russia. On 5 June it was noted on Crewe depot, prior to being towed to Cardiff and shipment later in the month. Since then little has been heard of it and it is assumed that it was dismantled for analysis of its technology; certainly Brush never supplied any spares subsequent to its despatch.

In terms of available power *Kestrel* was ahead of its time by about 10 years; certainly today it could have been fully utilised. This meant that its components were not tested to the limits. It would have been interesting to see how the 16LVA24 diesel engine would have performed, given the poor experience BR had with the similar 12LVA units fitted to five Brush Type 4s, Class 48. English Electric acquired the UK manufacturing rights in 1969, presumably to save development work on its CSVT range, but despite putting in some research into the use of a cast iron crankcase, nothing has come of the licensing deal. It served as an excellent demonstrator and proving ground for the Brush ac/dc power equipment, traction motors and electronic control gear and helped win Brush the order for its use in Class 56. Nothing, though, is ever said of the dynamic brake and inertia filtration systems so it is not possible to gauge their success. Both contributed to a heavier locomotive and neither have subsequently found favour in BR use, except for continued inclusion of dynamic brake gear in new designs of ac electric locomotives. Some facets of the design were not ideal but this is only to be expected in any prototype. The bogies did not give more than an acceptable ride at high speed, but lessons learned have since stood both Brush and BR in good stead with the Type 5 freight locomotives and also the IC125 power cars.

Right:
**With a view to assessing
the main equipment to be
used in the new freight
design, Class 56, a
Class 47 was converted
by fitting a Ruston 16
cylinder RK diesel and
Brush ac power
generation equipment.
Numbered No 47601 it
was based at Tinsley and
worked coal traffic in the
area. It was subsequently
fitted with the Ruston
12-cylinder version of the
RK engine, for service
trials in anticipation of
Class 58. No 47901 spent
most of the 1980s
allocated to Bristol Bath
Road. Indeed, some might
say it spent most of its
time *on* the depot under
repair! This was due to
problems obtaining some
spares and the technical
problems mentioned in
the text. It is seen here 'at
home' on 2 June 1987.**
M. Goodfield

Left:
**During December 1987
No 47901 was shopped at
Doncaster for an F exam,
emerging in Railfreight
sectorised livery. Very
soon after its release it
was recorded on
17 March 1988 between
Great Elm and Badlam
Tunnels near Frome with
the 12.09 Whatley
Quarry-Fareham.**
M. G. Miller

CHAPTER 3

The Type 5 Prototype

HS4000 *Kestrel* had barely been sold abroad when changing events on the world stage brought about a revised requirement on BR for freight motive power. The oil crisis of 1972/73, with spiralling prices and concern over supply called into question the strategic wisdom of its use as a main fuel source for the CEGB. A political decision was therefore taken to switch CEGB sourcing in favour of indigenous coal; this entailed an increase in block train movements. During the 1960s, not long after MGR-type workings started, Class 47s began to suffer, in particular, main generator failures due to being worked for too long a period outside the continuous rating limits of the electrical machines as mentioned in Chapter 1. Obviously the extra traffic could not be transported in longer trains and with no spare capacity within the Class 47 fleet to meet this upsurge in demand a swift solution in terms of new locomotives was the only answer.

An additional difficulty was that the BR workshops considered they would not have sufficient capacity, due to ongoing repair programmes, to meet the delivery dates required. The Board therefore put out tenders to interested parties, both at home and abroad. By now, however, there was very little capacity for locomotive construction left within Britain, the manufacturers, such as Brush and EE, which had built locomotives in the 1960s, having curtailed these operations in the face of no more foreseeable orders from the home market. Interest worldwide in *Kestrel* had, however, seen Brush establish a close relationship with the Rumanian locomotive industry and this was to enable the company to win the order for the first batch of new diesels.

It seems that a vague business specification was produced for the new fleet and, due to the haste, the detailed design work was ill-considered and this has since caused problems. What was required was a prime mover of around 3,000bhp to 3,500bhp, capable of hauling both heavy, low-speed coal trains and high-speed (80mph) liner traffic. It seems clear that BR realised that the 4,000hp capability of *Kestrel* was not needed. A 21-ton axle loading was specified. BR was happy with the service experience demonstrated by the EE 16CSVT fitted to Class 50 and the subsequent work which GEC had carried out to improve further its design and performance. The Board was also pleased with the Brush ac power generation equipment. The result was a locomotive design based largely on the Class 47 body, though stretched to the same length as *Kestrel*, using similar electrical machines and electronics to those of the latter but with a Ruston 16RK3CT power plant.

Before going on to consider the application of the foregoing features in a demonstrator for the proposed Type 5 freight class it is worth examining the refinements that had brought the EE diesel from a 1,600bhp unit, as used in the LMS Nos 10000/1 to one rated at 3,500bhp. During the 1950s EE had spent considerable sums in attempting to produce a new range of engines to replace its RK range, which had first seen rail use in 1933 in the 350bhp LMS standard shunter. Unfortunately the effort proved fruitless and, in order to meet the needs of higher power being sought around the world by railway operators, a rather low budget scheme to update the SVT engine was put in hand. This saw the application of charge air cooling and first use was made in the 12-cylinder version for both East Africa and the BR Type 3 (later Class 37). By virtue of its age and design, though, the RK range was considered as crude and cheap by BR, which opted instead, when it came to a diesel engine to power its new Type 4, for the more sophisticated Sulzer 12LDA28, rated at 2,750bhp.

Perhaps because there seemed little prospect of future orders for the 16CSVT, and also seemingly because of internal EE politics over who should pay for development costs, no further major work was done on the RK range during the first half of the 1960s. Most notable here was the retention of chain drive for the camshafts. Thus when the Class 50 order came EE could not offer a diesel engine in 1966 which was as modern as the Sulzer unit used in the 'Peaks' and Brush Type 4 some five years earlier. In 1966 EE took over Ruston & Hornsby, incorporating Davey-Paxman, and so attention switched instead to developing a diesel range based on the Paxman Ventura. Acquisition of the UK licence to manufacture the Sulzer 16LVA24 saw time, effort and money ploughed into this project but, again, to no avail and by 1970 it seems EE, by then part of GEC, reverted to the RK diesel and gave it a thorough redesign.

Out went the chain drive, replaced by gear drive for the camshafts. To accommodate the gear drive the crankcase and bed plates were redesigned and also strengthened to cope with the higher peak cylinder pressure coming with greater power. A Mk 3 version of cylinder head was produced, and fitted. Other modifications saw a new type of Napier turbocharger introduced which meant that only two, instead of four, were needed and oil-cooled pistons were fitted. Overall, the revision enabled output to be raised to 3,520bhp at 900rpm, though for BR use a figure of 3,250bhp was adopted.

With a view to achieving some preproduction running with the main components intended for Class 56, as the new class was to become, it was decided to re-equip a Class 47 to serve as a mobile testbed. As Class 47 No 47046 had been out of service in Crewe works following derailment damage sustained north of Peterborough on 29 September 1974, it was selected for the purpose. Accommodating the 16RK3CT diesel and alternator posed some problems, being larger than the power unit it replaced, and this caused some delay, so that service running did not actually begin until Class 56 had arrived. To dissipate the extra heat generated by the engine a revised cooler group was called for. Other changes internally included the fitting of a fresh electronic load regulator and a TD automatic voltage regulator, whilst the Davies & Metcalfe E70 type of brake unit, with centralised electrical control, was installed.

Further changes were to be found with the bogies. Essentially these were of the standard Class 47 pattern, retaining the same traction motors and gearing for 95mph, rather than 80mph, as had been decided upon for Class 56. Whereas a Class 56 motor has a continuous rating of 900A, the Class 47-type are only rated at 710A. Thus quite a lot more current would have to be absorbed and without any form of overload protection. Even so, generally speaking the motors have not given trouble. Unlike most of Class 47, which has traction motors connected in all-parallel, the conversion was to have its motors configured in series-parallel, as for Class 56. Speed sensing differed, the Hawker Siddeley electronic unit being replaced by a modular unit of Brush design. In order to obtain high adhesion it was deemed necessary to fit medium-speed sanders to the bogies and this brought about the relocation of the brake return springs.

During December 1975 renumbering to No 47601 took place and, when ready to return to service, the locomotive was reallocated to Tinsley, where the first Class 56s would go. It was demonstrated there, in the company of one of the latter, on 9 November 1976. Regrettably, it is not possible to quote the date of return to traffic; two sources give December 1975 but reports from Crewe during the early part of 1976 show it was still

Above:
After conversion from a standard Class 47, No 47601 worked off Tinsley depot. On 28 February 1977 it is seen heading south between Treeton Sidings and Beighton, Sheffield.
L. A. Nixon

Right:
**Construction of Class 56 was split between three workshops.
Nos 56001-30 came from Rumania, Nos 56031-115 originated at Doncaster and Nos 56116-135 were products of Crewe. By 18 June 1978, when this shot was taken, the Class 56 building programme at Doncaster was well under way. No 56050 is the example seen here in primer.**
C. R. Holland

Left:
The main factor influencing the decision to order the class was the oil crisis of the early 1970s, which brought increased block coal movements by rail. The power stations in the Trent Valley, served by ER depots such as Shirebrook and Worksop, were the first to see Class 56 on their services. High Marnham was one of these and this photograph, dated 30 April 1981, depicts the power station and No 56084, the first to receive the revised large-logo style of livery from new. *C. R. Holland*

there in April. Although a hybrid of two standard types, the drivers' union insisted on a full week's driver training conversion course and this made it unpopular with the ER Operating Department which would only pay for Tinsley men to receive training. This served to restrict No 47601 to out-and-back turns from Tinsley and reduced the flexibility of its use. Records of actual work are scarce, but most of the time it seems to have been hauling coal trains around South Yorkshire, North Nottinghamshire and Derbyshire. When the time came for it to be converted to house the new Ruston diesel, intended for the Class 58 design then being conceived, the ER declined to take it and so a new home on the WR was found. No 47601 re-entered Crewe works in September 1978 and so had seen less than two years' service. It had been converted from a standard Class 47 to act as a proving ground for some of the features specified for Class 56, but the conversion work had taken so long that its entry into traffic was virtually simultaneous with, rather than ahead of, the new fleet and so this purpose was not met.

The Class 58 project came into being in 1978 but whether this was the factor which influenced the second re-engining of the locomotive is uncertain as Ruston was now able to offer the RKCT in 12-cylinder form and the company may have been keen to demonstrate its capabilities. Further development work had produced a diesel capable of 3,500bhp at 1,000rpm but from four fewer cylinders than before. This was achieved still using the same size cylinder as that first applied in 1933 in the LMS shunter but now each produced 291.6hp, against 58.3 in the 1933 version, a fivefold increase in power. Fewer cylinders means less maintenance and a lower fuel consumption was also achieved. Whatever the motivation for the second conversion, No 47901 (renumbering coming in November 1979) was not released from Crewe works, where the work was again carried out, until December 1979. During tests in the works excessively high engine room temperatures were recorded, bringing the need for covered louvres to be fitted in the roof at both ends of the engine. A further modification was the fitting of a headlight in each cab front. Instead of going straight to traffic it went to the Railway Technical Centre (RTC) at Derby but, rather embarrassingly, the diesel engine suffered a camshaft cover failure in January 1980 and this necessitated a hasty return to Crewe for repair. For service use the diesel was rated at 3,300bhp.

Outshopped on 30 May and returned to traffic for the second time on 13 June, the LMR 'borrowed' it for a few days, as it was noted on Mollington Street depot, Birkenhead. By 19 June, however, it had reached its new home depot at Cardiff Canton and was sent to Margam for crew training. A handful of turns from here were to be covered, primarily to Trostre and Velindre, thus economising on the number of drivers requiring training. Changing patterns of steel traffic brought this use to a swift end and from 1 July No 47901 moved to Ebbw Junction to cover coal movements out of Cardiff Tidal Sidings and Newport Docks. Being equal to a Class 56 it took its turn hauling the trains to Didcot power station, a trial run with 45 46-tonne HAA wagons being made in September. During the period of crew training it saw use as the bank engine, piloting the Didcot workings out of the Severn Tunnel as far as Stoke Gifford. By January 1981 training of Swindon crews meant No 47901 could be diagrammed on any of the three MGR trains from South Wales to Didcot.

Coal importation through South Wales ports for Didcot came to an end in the summer, due to union opposition, and on 24 August No 47901 reverted to steel traffic, though still at Ebbw Junction; this entailed tripping between Llanwern and Pengam to Ebbw Vale. A new traffic flow of steel for export through Harwich brought a visit to Temple Mills yard in East London four days later but, again, this flow was short-lived. On 1 September a shortage of Class 47s found it hauling the Pengam-Southampton Freightliner.

Without the ability to work in multiple with a Class 56, No 47901 was unsuitable for the iron ore turns between Port Talbot and Llanwern. Although still outstationed and manned at Ebbw Junction, a change of scene came from February 1982 when it began to take a hand in the ARC stone trains from Tytherington quarry near Bristol to Wolverton; Swindon men, already trained from the days of the Didcot runs, took it forward from their home depot. Whilst at Ebbw Junction, a decision was taken to rerate the diesel to the manufacturer's rating of 3,500bhp, this being done statically, rather than on Canton load bank. The locomotive ran successfully in this form until a piston change several years later. From 3 October, a further move saw reallocation to Bristol Bath Road depot and outstationing at Westbury for diagramming on the stone traffic from Merehead quarry. Although the arrival of Foster Yeoman's Class 59s in March 1986 brought a slight change, it is still to be found at Westbury (unless under repair at Canton, to where it was reallocated from November 1987 after the Railfreight Sector pulled out of Bath Road), although now hauling ARC wagons from Whatley quarry.

The locomotive has remained a developmental vehicle, even though it has more than once been written off for this purpose. Ruston was surprised that the diesel gave no trouble at a time when the Class 58 fleet was plagued with piston failures. Eventually Ruston requested the pistons be removed for examination and so in May 1986 No 47901 was towed to Toton for the exchange, with a visit to Doncaster works for running-in afterwards. The major source of trouble has been with engine pipework which has been prone to failure. It is not unique in this respect, the Class 56 fleet being similarly afflicted. Being nonstandard, even as regards Class 58 (which have engines with only one, instead of two turbochargers and a different governor), many components have to be made as one-offs and this causes delay in repair. Hence a failure can result in abnormally long periods out of traffic. It has, however, proved more reliable than a WR Class 56 on similar work. Clearly Railfreight has faith in its worth. It is now nominally limited to a 75mph maximum speed and is currently allocated to the Aggregates sub-Sector, Cardiff pool.

CHAPTER 4

Class 56 — Design and Service Experience

The origins of this design have been traced in Chapter 3 dealing with No 47601. In 1974 the BRB realised it had neither the design resources nor production capability to get the proposed Type 5 from drawing board to finished product in the required timescale. Accordingly a broad specification was sent to a number of interested parties for them to submit tenders for evaluation by the Board. The one which resulted in an order, placed incidentally in September 1974, came from Brush. It was an amalgam of components which had already seen use on BR before. The basic structure was essentially a Class 47 body. An improved and uprated version of the EE 16CSVT diesel engine (used in Class 50) was a sensible choice and this was matched with Brush ac power generating equipment, as proved in *Kestrel* and already planned for the IC125 Class 43 power cars. With control equipment that is virtually identical (Class 56 is wired for six, rather than four traction motors), identical E70 brake unit and cab air-conditioning module, the Class 56 can be considered as a freight version of the Class 43 power car.

Ironically, this brought together in a single design the products of the two old rivals, Brush and EE. Following the sale of *Kestrel* to Russia, Brush had developed links with Electroputere of Craiova, Rumania with a view to the design and production of a range of locomotives. Brush could therefore arrange for manufacture of the new locomotives under this collaborative agreement to an acceptable timescale. For the government of the day the contribution of 70% of the components from Britain and the linking of this order to a Rumanian business within a larger bilateral trade deal including British aircraft exports, presented no problems and so the project went ahead.

The basic body shell is of monocoque construction, with stressed skin bodysides. It is capable of withstanding a 200-ton load on the buffer beams. An all-steel roof has doors to give access to the engine for component removal; the entire roof is detachable to allow the power unit to be removed. Bulkheads divide the body internally into three compartments for the cooler group, engine room and auxiliary and control equipment. Driving cabs of aluminium construction have a driver's desk which is very similar to that of the Class 47. In line with the IC125 power cars then under construction, the cabs were fitted new with air conditioning. This was found to be a less desirable option than an efficient pressure ventilation system for a locomotive engaged in shunting moves and so, from No 56091 onwards, this latter form of heating and ventilation was adopted. This modification will be dealt with in more detail later.

The internal layout of the design can be seen in Figure 3. At No 1 end is the cooler group which consists of two separate cooling systems. One cools the engine block and turbochargers, the other cools the charge air coolers and engine oil. A 19gal header tank feeds both systems, with a sight glass showing the contents. Each cooling water circuit has its own hydrostatic controller. These controllers operate through a flow valve which determines the flow of hydrostatic oil from a single hydrostatic pump to the two radiator fan motors. This means either of the hydrostatic controllers can activate operation of the roof-mounted radiator fan, depending on which cooling water system reaches the temperature setting of the hydrostatic controller first. The hydrostatic pump is itself driven by a shaft from the free end of the engine.

Right:
Until its closure in the early 1980s, Wath yard (electrified as part of the Woodhead scheme at 1,500V dc) was an important centre for MGR coal. Depot and footplate staff here were among the first to be trained on Class 56. No 56034, in original all-blue style, departs for Cudworth on 13 August 1980.
A. O. Wynn

Left:
With the closure of Wath, Doncaster depot became responsible for most of its work and has continued to be an important centre for MGR movements. No 56074 was the first of the class to be named, receiving *Kellingley Colliery* plates on 14 June 1982. In this August 1982 picture, its pristine condition is still evident, the grey roof being very unusual for an all-blue bodyside paint scheme. Note also the orange warning light on the cab roof, fitted as part of the remote control trials described in Chapter 4. Doncaster is the location.
David N. Clough

**Figure 3: Class 56
General Arrangement**

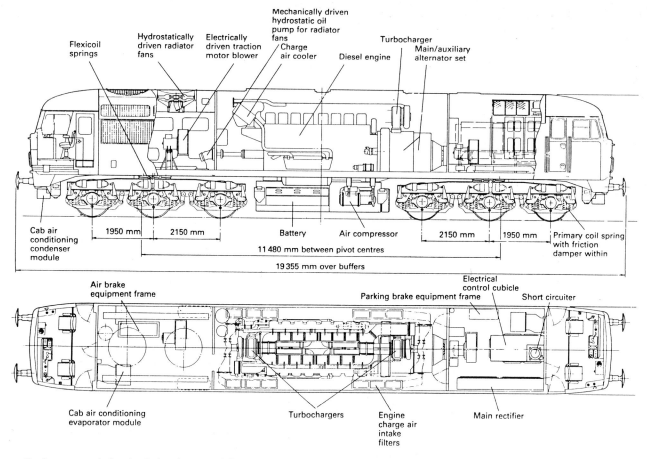

Radiator panels in single bank assemblies are on either side of the locomotive, each cooling water circuit has its own set of elements. As compared to Class 47, the capacity of the system is greater in order to absorb the extra heat generated by a more powerful diesel. Although the class has a service rating of 3,250bhp, the nominal rating of 3,520bhp was used when account was taken of the amount of heat to be dissipated. Main air reservoirs, the brake equipment frame, a traction motor

blower and the cab-heating unit are also located in this compartment. The Davies & Metcalfe E70 electronic brake module is included.

In the engine room there is a single Ruston 16 RK3CT diesel, fitted with two turbochargers and intercoolers. Although the manufacturers offer the unit at 3,520bhp, for BR use it delivers 3,250bhp at 900rpm. A Brush BA1101A main alternator is coupled directly to the engine crankshaft and is a 12-pole, three-phase brushless machine, demonstrating the progress made in the field of electronics since the mid-1960s, whereas *Kestrel* used 84 diodes in its main rectifier, the model used in Class 56 only has 36. After its output has been rectified it is rated at 840V/2,730A or 1,520V/1,520A continuously or 760V/3,000A for 1hr. The Brush auxiliary alternator of Type BAA602A is also mounted on the engine crankshaft and is an eight-pole, three-phase machine.

At No 2 end is the clean air compartment. This contains the control equipment cubicle, main rectifier, battery charge equipment, a second cab heating unit, traction motor blower for No 2 end bogie, auxiliary air reservoir and brake equipment frame for the parking brake. A fully electronic control system is used. Underslung beneath the locomotive and between the bogies are the fuel tank, batteries, air compressors and air reservoirs, spillage drain tank and four sandboxes; four more are fitted at the outer corners of the underframe.

The bogie has a main frame made up of two welded box sections and is designated CP2. It is derived from one of Swiss origin. As part of a design process to produce a new standard bogie, No 56042 was fitted with a set of bogies of different type, CP1. Savings in manufacturing and running costs were aimed for and lessons learned were incorporated in the CP3 bogie fitted to Class 58. Each bogie has three Brush TM73-62 traction motors mounted one to each axle. These motors are series wound, force-ventilated machines and are derived from the successful TM73-68 Mk 3 motors used in Class 46. Among the differences are changes in design to absorb the higher current. Continuous rating is 420V/910A and a single stage of field weakening is employed, taking place at 48mph. The motors are connected in series-parallel and drive the axles using a gear ratio of 16:63. Wheelslip detection is based on a voltage balance system and tractive effort is wound off automatically by the electronic control system in the event of prolonged slipping until the difference in voltage between slipping and non-slipping motors is eliminated. A proportion of the previous level of power is then reapplied and gradually increased to that selected by the driver. Manual sanding, by means of a button in the power handle, is available.

Driving controls are laid out in a similar way to Class 47. There is a combined master controller (for Engine Only, Forward, Reverse and Off) and power controller. Separate controls are provided for locomotive and train air braking; no provision for vacuum braking is included. As part of the (then current) practice towards fully-fitted freight trains, which entailed the guard travelling in the rear cab of the locomotive, a telephone handset is fitted in each cab to allow communication between the two.

Trailing 26 HAA wagons, No 56001 made its inaugural run on 24 September 1976, travelling from Treeton Junction, Sheffield to Appleby. This illustrates the run at Skipton.
Brian Morrison

Right:
From May 1981 Knottingley's diagrams went over to Class 56. The bulk of the work is in serving the power stations in the Aire Valley. Whilst most of the coal originates from Yorkshire mines, some is shipped from the North East. The usual arrangement is for a locomotive to bring a loaded train as far as York, then return north with empties. A Knottingley man then brings empties to York, before returning to one of the Aire Valley power stations with the loaded working. No 56103 curves south round the York avoiding line with a loaded train bound for the Aire Valley.
D. I. Rapson

Left:
**Gateshead had an
allocation of 24
locomotives until
October 1987 for use on
both coal and oil traffic in
the North East. Although
now based at Toton, the
work of the class in this
region remains
undiminished. There are
very few workings which
take this small fleet south
of York. One example,
though, is the Cawoods
export coal working, the
09.55 Blyth West TC-
Ellesmere Port. In this
shot, taken at King
Edward Bridge Junction,
Gateshead on 24 June
1988, No 56125 heads
south. Built in July 1983,
it has obviously taken
over four years for
No 56125 to reach
7,200hr and its first
F exam, when the Sector
livery would have been
applied.** *Peter J. Robinson*

Right:
**On 13 October 1984,
Nos 56047 and 56039
approach Bristol Temple
Meads.** *C. R. Holland*

Slow speed control at 0.5, 1 and 2.7mph is available and AWS, DSD and driver's vigilance devices are included. Multiple-unit connecting and control equipment allows up to three of the class, or Class 58, to be driven from one cab.

Details of dimensions can be found in the appendix at the end of the book. The overall weight of 126 tonnes is acceptable for the 80mph top speed, giving an axle load of 21 tonnes. The performance curve shows that the design is, to some extent, still a compromise. It was conceived as a stopgap until a full redesign of a Type 5 freight prime mover could be put in hand. It was intended, therefore, to be used on not only heavy block coal transfers between colliery and power station, but also to pull 75mph Freightliners. This explains the maximum service speed of 80mph and (relatively high) continuous rating speed of 17mph. Full power is available between 16mph and 81mph. Further, the maximum tractive effort of 61,000lb is not particularly high, considering the type of work on which the class would be deployed, being limited by the electrical equipment and the maximum adhesion possible. Indeed, it would have been better to have opted for a lower gearing to bring down both the speed at which full power can be developed and the continuous rating held. At the

continuous rating speed, a tractive effort of 54,000lb is available, which is more in line with what might be expected from a unit with a nominal rating of 3,250bhp.

Construction of the first 30 was carried out in Rumania, as Lot 1507 using components shipped from Britain. The second batch, Nos 56031-60 were built as Lot 1508 at BREL Doncaster although the bogies for them were also built in Rumania. The techniques used in Rumania did not produce the same standard of finished product as would be expected in this country. Welds were not finished off properly and gas piping was used for cable conduit. Worse still was the fact that brass collars were not fitted to the ends of this piping, leaving just a rough edge which could chafe the wires and cause earth faults. Whereas in this country copper is used for air pipes, mild steel was used in Rumania. It seems jig assembly was not used, as there was a lack of uniformity in assembly which meant, say, a section of pipework from one locomotive would not fit in the same place on a second locomotive. The stressed skin bodysides had not been finished off properly and ripples were clearly evident in the side panels. These are examples of some of the problems faced by Brush engineers who had to prepare the imports for commissioning.

The building programme at Doncaster was not all plain sailing either. With full capacity within the works and still shortages in metalworking and fabrication trades, normal practice in BREL led to some components being manufactured at other BREL workshops. Thus Swindon supplied radiator housings, internal doors, air ducting and spillage tanks, Ashford the roof sections, exterior doors and fuel tanks and Eastleigh the cab desks. For Doncaster's second batch of 30 locomotives, Nos 56061-90 (Lot 1509), Derby supplied the bogies, with Crewe manufacturing those for the remainder of the class. To enable the first pair of Derby-built bogies to be proved in service as soon as possible, they were fitted under No 56058; the last pair of Rumanian-built ones thus went under No 56061.

Arising in part out of this need for internal subcontracting and also with a view to reducing construction costs, the Doncaster Works Value Engineering Committee explored ways of reducing costs and came up with several revisions. Externally the most obvious is in the change from an aluminium cab unit to an all-steel one, as this was accompanied by a slight change in profile; this is visible by the cab front grille protruding rather than being flush. The change in profile of the steel cabs eliminated multiple bends and, by using single bends, was cheaper to produce. No 56056 was the first to have the new arrangement although No 56058/9 were built with alloy cabs, whilst No 56063 has one alloy and one steel cab. Fabricated cab exterior doors were replaced with an aluminium casting whilst the aluminium cab desk was changed to one of glass reinforced plastic (GRP) at the same time. The original roof was a single skin GRP dome, with insulation and interior cladding fitted during building. A double skin dome, moulded in one piece, was substituted from either No 56063 or No 56064, as spares of the first type, built as part of Lot 1508, were used up; the types are interchangeable.

From new Nos 56073-4 had equipment installed to facilitate remote operation during unloading at Eggborough power station. One aerial was mounted under the bogies, opposite the AWS receiver, and one at cantrail level. The equipment fitted had previously seen trial in Nos 47277 and 47373 and the change allowed the trials at Eggborough to continue. To highlight their presence they also received roof-mounted external orange flashing lights. After an extended trial the equipment was removed as it had been superseded by radio control. Nos 56116-135 were built new to accept radio control but union opposition has prevented widespread use. Transponders were fitted to all the Healey Mills-allocated locomotives (Nos 56020-29/31-4/73/74) in connection with the in-motion weighing system installed experimentally at Drax power station. This was a forerunner of the Automatic Vehicle Identification system, currently being fitted to MGR wagons and Coal Sector locomotives.

At Doncaster building commenced with the fabrication of the underframe from five jig-built box section sub-sections. Next, the jig-built bodyside frameworks were attached to the underframe and the bodyside skin attached. With the bodysides tensioned, the bulkheads were welded into place. Then the locomotive was fitted out with power unit assembly, auxiliary equipment, wiring and pipework, the process being completed by final bodyside preparation and painting. On-works testing then took place to ensure that the electrical insulation was to specification, followed by load bank running before being allowed on to the main line for a high-speed trial run. Early examples were given a loaded high-speed run, hauling 800 tons at up to 75mph but this was changed later so that the unit ran light engine to either Tyne Yard or Peterborough. Finally, before being accepted for traffic, a MGR duty was covered, usually from South Yorkshire to Immingham, to establish full operating capability. Once Doncaster had become familiar with the work practices it was able to turn out 14 examples in the last nine months of 1979 and 16 per annum over the succeeding two years. Construction of the final batch of 20 (Nos 56116-35) was switched to Crewe as Doncaster geared up for Class 58 production, and deliveries to traffic continued at the same pace during 1983. It took, however, nearly 12 months to get the last seven into service and almost five months for the final three.

The standard rail blue livery was adopted, with black underframe, bogies and buffer beams. During 1978 the Design Panel was asked to investigate alternative schemes and eventually No 56036 was repainted at Stratford into what has since become known as the large logo and numbers style. Wraparound yellow cabs, with black windows, silver grey roof and a BR emblem the full height of the body eventually became the standard from No 56084-134. Sectorisation has brought with it two main changes to the paint scheme. Firstly, there was the Railfreight grey, initially without, but later with, a red stripe along the solebar; this was similar to the style adopted from new for Class 58 and it is a source of surprise that the final batch of Class 56 (save for No 56135 which did receive grey paint from new) was not similarly turned out new from Crewe. Then came the Railfreight livery revision in the autumn of 1987 when a three-tone grey scheme was adopted, incorporating sub-Sector stripes to denote the type of work a particular example is allocated to; No 56001 was given the honour

Right:
Plawsworth, Co Durham is the location where No 56062 was photographed on 13 May 1986 in charge of a Jarrow-bound tank train. *Peter J. Robinson*

Left:
The LMR received the early output from Doncaster works in 1977, again, primarily for block coal transits to Trent Valley power stations, served by motive power off Toton. In this view No 56069 is seen at Moira West Junction on 17 May 1985, heading for Rugeley power station.
A. O. Wynn

of being the first to be so turned out as part of the exhibition associated with the relaunch, held at Ripple Lane in October that year.

Some of the inadequacies found in the Rumanian batch have already been mentioned. Manufacturing and assembly defects affecting the bogies gave rise to difficulty in negotiating curved track due to the lateral rotational restraint brackets requiring modification. Some clearance between the bogie frame and the traction motors had to be machined. The axlebox end floats were incorrectly set and this caused one of the middle axles under No 56001 to seize on its trial run. In addition, it was subsequently found that the traction motor suspension tubes had excessive end float and this was rectified at Doncaster. The edges on the bogie frames had not been dressed and this would have led to fracturing. Arising out of this state of affairs all the imported bogies had to be removed from the early deliveries (work generally done at Stratford) and sent to the Electric Construction Co (a Hawker Siddeley subsidiary) in Wolverhampton for modification whilst Doncaster reset the end floats on the wheelsets.

In the early days some instances of traction motor pinions coming loose took place. A couple of modifications to the air management system were needed. Firstly, the crankcase breather was exhausting dirty, oily air into the traction motor blower (and hence the motors) at No 1 end; this flow was changed so that the air passed between the radiator panels on A side and out through the roof. To supply air to the blower at No 1 end a clean supply was drawn in at roof level. The blower at No 2 end is supplied from the clean air compartment. The impellers in the motor blowers have been prone to disintegrate, sending a cascade of bits into the motors. Drypack air filters, mounted at cantrail level, were found to lack rigidity and in consequence were changed for a type offering better self-support, although extra frame support was also provided. Whereas initially these were changed at C exam intervals, 1,200hr, due to the dusty environment in which the class operates, this interval was later reduced to every B exam, at 400hr intervals.

A long-standing problem has been to keep pipework sealed. Leaks of exhaust gases, coolant and hydrostatic oil have, even now, not been overcome satisfactorily. On-line failures due to low coolant have been reduced in three ways. Firstly, a bigger header tank means the supply is less likely to run out between checks. Secondly, the original sight glass was often difficult to read and so has been replaced by a gauge on the bottom of the tank. Finally, to tackle the cause of the coolant problems, hoses have been fitted in place of metal sleeves and rubber ring-type couplings, whilst new jointing material has been used in critical areas such as on radiator elements, the intercooler gallery rail, the cylinder head outlet pipes and at either end of the flexible transfer elbow between cylinder block and cylinder head. To overcome hydraulic system problems, caused by failure of the small bore solid piping, which run between the controllers and the flow valves, long flexible hoses are being fitted.

With Class 47 the driver gets a warning of low coolant some time before the level gets so low as to cause engine shutdown; with Class 56, the warning comes at the same time as shutdown, leaving no opportunity to plan a stop to either replenish the supply or summon assistance. In view of the failure record due to this problem, it is surprising that a modification has not been fitted to provide an early warning, especially when suitable equipment is already in use in another class. Failure of the exhaust manifold bellows in the early years brought a partial redesign of the exhaust pipe system to reduce the amount of vibration, which was causing the fracturing. In addition, thicker, two-ply bellows were fitted to extend life. Originally the bellows between the turbocharger exhaust outlet and the silencer inlet were made of fabric and were prone to failure. A thicker fabric with a heat shield was tried unsuccessfully, as the heat shield distorted and the thicker material could not be compressed sufficiently to make it gas tight. A cheaper version, made of stainless steel, was then substituted successfully. With a view to reducing the leakage of exhaust gas, joints in the system have been welded up wherever possible which helps keep them tight but hardly makes for ease of disassembly. In 1985 a 'Stop Leaks' campaign was introduced to try and combat the continuing difficulties faced in all the areas mentioned above. By the time this book appears the entire class should have received the modifications.

The diesel engine has not been entirely free of problems. Although it was thought that this aspect had been covered properly at the design stage, turbocharger surging still manifested itself under engine full load condition. A smaller diffuser was fitted and this still allows adequate engine performance with a margin of safety from surging. Some problems, particularly on later built examples, with camshaft failures have given rise to a possible question mark over the then current specification of the camshaft and muff coupling bolts. The cams were breaking up on their surfaces due to the high loadings around the small holes created in their surfaces when hardness tests were carried out at the factory; Ruston had to dress the areas round the holes. Due to the locomotives being worked harder on the WR, failures occurred first on that region. A further possibility was that the latter were being torque loaded to an excessive degree in the workshops during overhaul.

More recently, there have been instances of piston failure. Turbochargers have not tended to last longer than three to four years and No 56051 was tried with blowers of Brown-Boveri manufacture. For comparison, No 56001 received a set of Napier Mk 3 blowers and, for comparison with No 56051, in April 1985 this machine was sent to the WR to operate out of Westbury on the arduous stone diagrams. The new Napier equipment has continued to function well and in August 1986 No 56038 emerged from its overhaul at Crewe having been fitted with the same components. A much simpler and compact exhaust system was able to be fitted in consequence. To be fair, there has been no difference between the performance of the Napier Mk 3s and the Brown-Boveri ones. The extra size of the diesel over the Sulzer 12LDA28 means that the engine room is a very cramped place in which to carry out maintenance. One option being considered when the fleet comes up for mid-life overhaul is the fitting of a different engine to the 16RK3CT currently employed.

Ride quality is soft and has been the cause of complaint. Investigation has revealed the problem to be twofold. Firstly, when the diesel was running at around 580rpm the body structure was found to be very sensitive to the vibration frequencies and the cab floor would vibrate. A revised form of engine mounting was tried unsuccessfully and consideration given instead to a modification to the control system which would prevent the engine running at the critical speed. There was also intermittent banging from the bogies, caused by, in part, poor quality primary suspension springs. Those manufactured in Rumania had been hand wound and did not compress evenly under pressure. Substituting machine wound alternatives solved the problem.

Complaints concerning the cab-heating arrangements have been touched on earlier. Unlike the IC125 unit cab, there were many more times during a driver's turn of duty when the stable cab environment would be upset by having to open an external door or window. Further, the thermostat in the air-conditioning unit gave a preset temperature which was not to everyone's liking. This gave rise to some drivers tampering with the setting. In addition, the location of the unit in the cab was high in the rear bulkhead and this often caused drivers' legs and feet to be without heat and become cold during long spells at the controls. By virtue of the positioning of the external inlet, some drawing-in of exhaust from the diesel could happen. A metal cab, with little insulation, was neither conducive to warmth nor did it prove to be free of draughts. The winter of 1977/78 brought so many complaints that, at one stage, a blacking of the class was feared. Several measures were introduced to remedy the situation. An experiment on No 56067 saw engine coolant used as a means of supplying heat via a pressure ventilation system. From No 56091 onwards this was fitted as standard, with electric preheaters. Nos 56061-90 (excluding No 56067) have underfloor heating banks which can blow air into the driver's knee-hole position. As no 'off' position was available, overheating of the cab caused problems and this fitting of an 'off' switch was included in the modifications. The thermostat units have been resealed to make them tamper-proof and polyurethane foam was injected into the cab sealing skirt of the Rumanian-built units to give more effective sealing and insulation. These measures have now eradicated the problem.

Right:
A landfill project at Fletton, near Peterborough, provides BR with a traffic flow of fly ash from, among others, Ratcliffe power station in the Trent Valley. Once Class 56 had taken over the MGR duties to these power stations from Class 47, it was natural for them to also cover the fly ash traffic. No 56057, of Toton, passed Woodcroft Crossing on the approach to the East Coast main line at Werrington on 12 September 1981 with one such working.
C. R. Holland

Left:
Aggregates quarried in the East Midlands, Avon and Somerset give a lucrative source of business for the Railfreight sector. The LMR bases some of its fleet at Leicester to cover output from Bardon Hill and Mountsorrel quarries. The stone is shipped to a variety of depots, mainly in the Southeast. No 56058 was painted in the first version of Railfreight grey, without red at solebar level, when captured by the camera on 13 June 1987 at Thorney Mill terminal west of London. Bardon Hill is the source of the stone. *Brian Morrison*

CHAPTER 5

Class 56 — Allocation and Utilisation

By July 1976 Doncaster had laid down the frames for Nos 56031/2. On the fourth of the following month the first two Rumanian-built examples were unloaded at Harwich Parkeston Quay, moving to Tinsley on the seventh. As more arrived they were towed to Barrow Hill. On 25 November No 56002 was working a train through Featherstone and by the end of the month the distribution of the class was Nos 56001/4/7/8 at Tinsley, No 56002 at Knottingley, No 56003 at the Railway Technical Centre, Derby, Nos 56005/6/9/11 in Doncaster works and No 56010 in Derby works. The presence of No 56002 at Knottingley was for crew training and No 56006 went to Shirebrook in December for the same purpose. On the sixth of that month it had made a commissioning run from Treeton to Blea Moor, hauling 26 loaded hoppers, about 750 tonnes gross. Equally, No 56006 had made a trial run to Marsden and had restarted 1,200 tonnes on the 1 in 105 climb out of Huddersfield without difficulty. Although No 56031 was expected to be ready to leave Doncaster for trials by the end of the year, the date passed without it appearing.

Early in the month No 56014 arrived at Tinsley and was sent to Barrow Hill for storage, pending the commissioning of the earlier examples. This procedure was adopted for others of the class and Darnall provided similar accommodation. No 56001 took the 09.10 Broughton Lane-Peterborough carrying old rails up the East Coast main line on 22 February 1977; two days later No 56008 made a similar trip and this became a regular trial run for a while. BR finally accepted No 56001 into service on 28 February, nearly seven months since it docked at Harwich. With seven available for traffic by March the first revenue-earning trips were to High Marnham power station. In reality little time was saved by having the first 30 built abroad, for No 56031, the first of the Doncaster batch, was commissioned on 13 May and went to Toton later in the month for crew training. During the summer, visits were being made to Stratford for bogie exchanges, as mentioned in the previous chapter.

The honour of taking the first passenger train went to No 56008 which worked to Melton Mowbray on 24 July. Toton's allocation, comprising those built at Doncaster, soon began to appear at Fletton with fly ash from Ratcliffe and Drakelow power stations. During August crew training at Saltley got underway, firstly with No 56032, replaced later in the month by No 56033. The final Rumanian-built unit arrived on 20 August. A dispute by power station workers saw No 56019 despatched to Heaton depot for use as a standby generator. The LMR's allocation began work in the Birmingham area as part of the crew training exercise, but it was Tinsley-based No 56029 which was the first to appear at Three Spires when, on 12 October, it worked a coal train to Ironbridge power station. Generally speaking, it was MGR traffic out of Kingsbury (also to Ironbridge) which had a Class 56 in charge.

At the start of 1978 work at Doncaster had reached Nos 56040-9, with the former being painted. Later in January No 56034 spent some time at Coalville for trials. On 21 January No 56033 was used for high-speed ride tests between Duddeston and Basford Hall. Whilst 85% availability was expected, it was by no means always achieved and depots had to resort to Class 47s again when short. Wath and Doncaster crews had, by now, been trained. No 56038 was loaned to the WR for the same purpose. Banbury drivers began familiarisation around the same time so that the type could be diagrammed for the runs to Didcot power station. On 7 April No 56035 was the first to take a MGR train over this course. During May No 56043 went on loan to Reading in the same connection. Problems over manning the class delayed its takeover of the work from Class 47. No 56043 became the first to visit Bristol, a depot to which it would later be allocated, when it towed 'dead' Class 50 No 50047 there on 12 April. By May the '56s' had begun to take over at Coalville.

Yet another route was added to the widening sphere of the class when No 56042 hauled a Wellbeck-Northfleet duty as far as Brent on 10 July; a Derby test car was also in tow, so the run may have been part of a test of the CP1 bogies fitted to that machine. Willesden received a visit from No 56040 on 30 August. The transfer of four examples from Toton to Tinsley in October 1978 allowed the following diagrams to be covered, four off Tinsley, six off Barrow Hill, two off Worksop, 10 off Shirebrook, three off Wath and two off Doncaster depot. A portent of things to come was No 56022 turning up at Stanlow on 9 March 1979 with an oil train. It was not until the demise of Class 40 some six years later that Class 56 took over these duties. Trials with a 45-wagon train to Didcot on 31 May, with No 56035 in charge, were not successful due to problems inside the power station. By this time there were typically six Class 56 appearances here each day.

A regular practice in later years was the deployment of Type 5 freight power on Euston-Birmingham services, diverted via Nuneaton, from there into New Street. This seems to have taken place for the first time on 14 May 1979 when No 56053 took the 13.30 out of Birmingham. Whether this first instance was due to non-availability of a Class 47/4 is not known, but in later years this availability was not the factor in deciding what Control turned out for these duties. Later in the year on 17 December gales blew down the overhead lines north of Carlisle. Services were diverted via Newcastle and Berwick, with No 56065 having to be rostered on the 09.35 Euston-Inverness, presumably only as far as Edinburgh. As this locomotive had been making its way

to Scotland anyway for trials out of Hunterston it proved to be a convenient way of getting it there. On 28 November Paddington got its first Class 56 visit in the shape of No 56064 piloting two failed Class 47s on the 08.35 from Birmingham.

May 1979 saw plans for the wider use of the class on the LMR put in hand when No 56040 was sent to Cricklewood for training depot staff, with No 56049 arriving on 16 June for driver training. Often this would entail working the Brent-Stewartby refuse train, taking the class on to the Bedford to Bletchley line. On 18 August No 56040 ventured south of the Thames into Kent on a Northfleet coal train. By October sufficient drivers had been trained and so through working from Welbeck, with 43 HAAs, was instigated.

Preparatory for the allocation of some of the fleet to the WR, No 56036, in its revised livery, arrived at Cardiff Canton on 2 July, followed by No 56035 to Margam the next day. Both were for driver and depot training. On 24 July the latter appeared on Port Talbot-Velindre steel duties whilst next day both examples were tried on the 08.10 Port Talbot-Llanwern, operating in multiple. Effective from July 1979 some of Toton's allocation was moved to Canton, primarily to replace triple-headed Class 37s on the Port Talbot-Llanwern services; this involved working in pairs, almost certainly the first use of the multiple-unit facility on a regular basis. During August the temporary suspension of iron ore traffic resulted in them being switched to Margam to Trostre and Velindre steel traffic, together with oil from Llandarcy to Aberthaw, Llanwern and Ebbw Vale. Although the reason for its arrival at Hereford on 20 August is not recorded, No 56041 was the first to visit this locality.

Knottingley staff had been trained on Class 56 shortly after the latter arrived from Rumania. Due to the absence of a single manning agreement for the type at the time, coupled with all that depot's diagrams being operated on this basis, it was not until the new timetable came into force on 12 May 1980 that the Type 5s displaced Class 47 in the Aire Valley. As Knottingley was unable to carry out maintenance above a C exam, the locomotives were allocated to Healey Mills. The previous September saw

No 56031 appear in the area for driver training. It might appear that Class 56 has done virtually no high-speed freight work but this is not so. Proof of this was the regular use of a Canton unit on the 19.10 Pengam-Stratford Freightliner during December 1979 whilst East London was host to No 56069 on 21 December when it worked to Ripple Lane with the 01.01 liner ex-Nottingham.

In readiness for a new traffic flow between the steelworks at Llanwern and Shotton, crew training at Shrewsbury commenced late in 1979 and No 56064 was still there in February 1980. No 56033, transferred from Tinsley to Canton, was the first to reach Dee Marsh Junction on 13 June. Shrewsbury received a visit from another direction on 5 October arising out of engineering work between Rugby and Birmingham, when No 56063 took a diverted Euston train from Nuneaton.

September found more crew training taking place on the WR, this time at Newport Ebbw Junction; this was in readiness for coal importation through Newport and Cardiff bound for Didcot and No 56035 was involved. Swindon men also received training. When the service started it was not uncommon for a Class 56, or No 47901, to be used as pilot as far as Bristol Parkway, though a Type 3 could also be used. From December, though, Cardiff's allocation was reduced to six Class 56s, which were for use on the Danygraig-Stratford liner, the coal traffic to Didcot and iron ore service between Port Talbot and Llanwern. Once Hereford men had learnt the locomotives they were turned out on the Pengam-Glasgow Freightliner as far as Crewe, returning with the balancing working. Class 56s seem to have been allocated the work due to the extra tonnage being transported. Reliability was not all that it might have been and this led to problems when a failure did happen since there was no replacement Type 5 to deputise. Various combinations of traction would then have to substitute but the most interesting came in 1987 when the two Class 50s off the evening Paddington-Hereford services were jumpered together and took the north-bound train forward to cover a Class 56 failure, returning to Hereford with the up train in time for their respective morning duties to Paddington.

Far left:
The demise of Class 40 brought Class 56 in substitution as motive power for the oil traffic from Stanlow refinery. Its use on these trains proved to be transitory, for May 1987 brought a switch to Class 47. A number of depots on the ER and ScR, as well as the LMR, form the destinations for the refinery's output. On 24 February 1986 No 56058, in the first version of Railfreight grey paintwork, approaches Miles Platting with a Leeds-Stanlow service. The site of Brewery Sidings yard, closed in the early 1970s, can be seen to the left.
David N. Clough

Left:
No 56088 passes Melton Mowbray with the 08.29 ThFO Mountsorrel-Radlett Redland train on 8 August 1985.
A. O. Wynn

Although No 56006 had made a trial run to Marsden not long after it appeared on BR, 20 November 1980 witnessed a fresh set of tests with No 56032 trailing 32 wagons. This was a prelude to the class taking over responsibility for transporting coal from South Yorkshire to Fiddlers Ferry power station, this being prompted by the planned closure of the Woodhead route. It did not, though, prove to be plain sailing for train crews the following November, when several trains stuck at Golcar on wet rails made worse by fallen leaves. For example, on 14 November No 56046, trailing 32 wagons, needed rear end assistance from a following York to Liverpool passenger after stalling. Meanwhile on 20 February 1981 Healey Mills' No 56024 ran light to Thornaby for driver training. Doncaster was progressing well with the third batch, with Nos 56091-9 in various states of assembly during April 1981; also on works at this time was No 56018 which was receiving its first classified repair. September saw No 56009 on Wearside for training duties, in readiness to Gateshead receiving an allocation from 22 November. In October No 56027 was at Gateshead for the same purpose. Early duties seem to have been off Blyth and once based here they soon ventured north of the Border with the Morpeth to Oxwellmains cement.

A new traffic flow of export coal from Washwood Heath through Garston Dock produced No 56003 on 20 May; it was probably the inaugural visit of Class 56 to the area as well. Subsequently the shipment of coal this way made the type daily visitors, coming either from the Birmingham area or Nottinghamshire. By the end of January 1982 Doncaster had Nos 56104-10 under construction and the first of these made its heavy load trial on 11 February between Doncaster and Immingham. Another milestone was the arrival in late May of No 56033 on the works, the first Doncaster-built unit to undergo a classified repair some five years after being built. The periodicity of such maintenance had been planned as four years. Across at Crewe works, construction of the final 20 (reduced from 55 by the BRB's decision to specify Class 58 instead) commenced during the summer. No 56115, Doncaster's last, left the works during mid-December. Tinsley's allocation was usually outstationed at Barrow Hill, Shirebrook and Worksop where in early 1982 the daily diagrams required five, 16 and five respectively off each sub-depot. New territory was covered on 27 February with the arrival of Nos 56013/91 at Westbury, on loan from Tinsley, for training purposes, heralding their eventual takeover of Somerset stone movements. Initially eight locomotives, allocated to Bristol Bath Road, were needed. Later in the year that depot's allocation commenced duties out of Tytherington quarry, including, from 6 January 1983, runs to Wolverton.

Back on the LMR from September 1982 a Toton-based machine was allocated a diagram of two return trips between Fiddlers Ferry power station and Llandudno Junction transporting fly ash for use as road base on the A55 road improvement scheme. At the end of the week the Class 56 returned home via the Warrington Arpley to Toton Speedlink. Thornaby received fairly regular visits from the ER fleet for tyre turning and by 1983 Teesside freights to the Northwest, such as the 23.00 Tees-to-Runcorn tanks, were producing a Class 56. West Wales oil traffic began to see Class 56s from May 1983, after No 56037 had been involved in driver training at Llanelli in April. Stone traffic originating in the Westbury area continued to build up during the year, particularly out of Foster Yeoman's Merehead quarry, and by September double-headed Class 56s were taking 43 bogie hoppers on the run to Acton and Purfleet in Essex; weighing some 4,400 tonnes, these were the heaviest trains at the time anywhere on BR. With stone terminals at Botley and Eastleigh, Class 56 commenced to work on to the SR's Western Division in consequence. October saw a change on the LMR with pairs of Class 31s giving way to a single Class 56 on the Redland stone movements from Mountsorrel; the Tarmac aggregates flows leaving Cliffe Hill already had Type 5 power.

Moving into 1984 an interesting, albeit short-lived duty was the movement of hot oil from Stanlow to Tees. Two Class 56s took the loaded wagons as far as Healey Mills where they met a brace of Class 37s with the return empties and the motive power was exchanged. With Manchester drivers not knowing Class 56, Warrington men learned the road to Healey Mills. April found the last three under construction at Crewe. On the 14th No 56131 was used to pilot the 09.30 Crewe-Holyhead as its trial run. Such trips along the North Wales coast remained common whilst Crewe retained responsibility for works repair until summer 1988, having taken over the task from Doncaster during May 1987. The first half of the decade saw the class fall well below its availability and reliability targets. It was fairly typical for only around 55% to be in traffic, whilst miles per casualty fluctuated around the 7,000 to 8,000 mark. Generally the ER fared better than the other two Regions. It was this state of affairs that brought the 'Stop Leaks' campaign and associated modifications. By 1988 matters had improved and 70% availability was invariably held or bettered. Two other items worthy of mention during 1984 were the training of SR drivers at Hither Green on the class during the summer (in connection with through freight movements from both the LMR and WR) and the emergence of No 56135 from Crewe, painted in Class 58-style Railfreight colours.

By now the pattern of utilisation had become pretty well established. The main duties allocated to the class have been described above but there were, of course, others. For example, the Teesside area saw quite a lot of freight moved by them and this included visits to Redmire. In addition to the coal movements between the Northeast and the South Yorkshire power stations there were many appearances on other duties. At weekends examples off Knottingley would be drafted on to engineers' trains. With the rundown of Class 40, a Class 56 which had reached the area on an oil train from the Northeast would cover a Warrington-Stanlow trip diagram. Oil services through Immingham could produce a Class 56.

The impact of Sectorisation began to have more effect during 1986/87 with the allocation of locomotives to sub-Sectors and a gradual drift towards only two depots having any on their books. The latter was due to Railfreight pulling out of Bath Road, with No 47901 and its stud of Class 56s used on stone traffic out of Tytherington and the Westbury area going to Canton. Gradually the ER's Type 5s were concentrated on Toton, with Gateshead's stock of 24 being the last to go, the move being effective from 5 October 1987. Sub-Sector allocation during that month was as follows:

FALX (stone — Leicester) Nos 56058-65
FANC (stone — Cardiff) Nos 56001/31-4/7-41/3/5/6/9/57
FBYB (coal — Blyth) Nos 56112-35
FHYU (coal — York) Nos 56002-30/42/4/7/54/66-111
FMCS (steel — Cardiff) Nos 56050/5/6
FPLW (oil — South Wales) Nos 56035/6/48

It is clear from the above just what type and volume of freight haulage Class 56 covers. Although, at first, there was some switching between sub-Sectors, this is now strictly controlled. This applies, even following a visit to Toton for routine examinations; C exams and above involve that depot's fleet returning to base and, as a C exam is every 1,200 TOPS hr, this arises, on average, every eight to nine months.

The first place where the dedicated fleet concept was brought in was Leicester from May 1987 when Nos 56058-64 were received, increased later by the addition of Nos 56065/70. A booming construction industry, especially in the Southeast, has seen continued growth in the aggregates flows out of Mountsorrel, Cliffe Hill and Bardon Hill, mostly destined for the Southeast but particularly depots around London. Normally the trains are formed of 42 PGAs, grossing 2,200 tonnes. This same increase in stone movements has now led the WR to redeploy its fleet entirely to the sub-Sector, leaving steel with Class 37/7 and 37/9. Certainly during 1988 there was a shortage of Type 5 capacity across BR as a whole.

By far the biggest allocation of Class 56 is to Yorkshire Coal, which, as noted above, had 99 engines in October 1987. Main deployment is to fuel the four power stations in the area, Drax, Eggborough, Ferrybridge and Thorpe Marsh, which take in total 535,000 tonnes of coal each week. This fleet usually works off Knottingley, Shirebrook and Worksop and also serves collieries and power stations in North Nottinghamshire and Lincolnshire. Other associated traffic flows are coking coal to Scunthorpe from Yorkshire, Betteshanger and Oakdale and the Blue Circle deliveries from Grimethorpe to Northfleet and Hope.

Right:
A little-photographed service involving a Midland Class 56 (for a short time a Class 58) is the cement working from Penyffordd in Clywd to Curzon Street. On 14 August 1985 No 56063 passes Hope on the Wrexham, Mold & Connahs Quay line with 6J65 12.45 Curzon Street to Penyffordd.
D. I. Rapson

Left:
The WR first received an allocation for use on the steel traffic, primarily ore trains from Port Talbot to Llanwern. Movement of finished steel has also been allocated to the class. Livery contrast of the large-logo and Railfreight grey styles are represented here by Nos 56048/050. They are heading the 14.45 Llanwern-Port Talbot iron ore empties on 19 September 1986, approaching Margam yard. *John Chalcraft*

The Northeast retains 24 of the class for work both north and south of the Tyne. Coal is, again, the main traffic, with six trains out of Seaham as well as Durham and Wearmouth to Sunderland South Dock and Westoe. Some of Durham's output is hauled up the main line to York for onward transit to the Aire Valley by Knottingley men. Butterwell despatches two trains to Wilton, with Blyth staithes and Tyne coal terminal also being destinations for Northumberland coal. A couple of oil trains are also programmed for the class off Thornaby.

Class 56 was conceived to meet the increasing demand for the shipment of coal to power stations in heavier trainloads than Class 47 could cope with. When MGR trains were introduced, their 1,650-tonne loads proved beyond the continuous rating for the latter type and this had led to many main generator failures; trailing loads had therefore been cut to 1,380 tonnes. Just how much better the lower gearing, coupled with sanding for poor rail conditions, built into Class 56 has been is demonstrated from the following:

Maximum Trailing Tonnages For MGR Location

	Class 47	Class 56
Woodhouse Junction-Worksop	1,200	1,640

For Class 47 the limit is imposed for continuous rating purposes whilst for Class 56 it is adhesion at starting which limits the train weight. In this respect, therefore, the Type 5 has met its design criteria.

The increasing trend towards CEM (variously described as Cost Effective or Component Exchange Maintenance) has brought the F and G exam as replacement for the former Light and Intermediate classified repair, the former done on depot, the latter on works. Due to it having spare capacity, Landore has taken a hand at carrying out F exams on the fleet whilst the transfer of Doncaster works from BREL ownership to become part of BRML has seen it become involved again with the class as it too performs F exams. Some idea of the reduced level of routine maintenance is evidenced by the following examination intervals:

Exam (Hours)	A	B	C	D
Class 47	55	275	825	1,650
Class 56	80	400	1,200	3,600

Just how this translates into lower maintenance is shown below, together with the volume of other repair work, expressed in standard hours per vehicle:

Work Type	Exam Work	Repair Work
Class 47	124	546
Class 56	119	494

Class 56 was conceived in a hurry and a price has had to be paid for this haste. Granted the class is better at hauling heavy freight than any of the mixed traffic Type 4s, not just because of its extra power but also arising from the '56s' being equipped and geared for that purpose. But that is only half the story and perhaps the best way to sum up the class is to quote the words of Messrs Russell & Brown of the Railway Technical Centre, who delivered a paper to the international conference, *Diesel Locomotives for The Future*, which was reproduced in the proceedings of the Institution of Mechanical Engineers: 'The early promise expected of this class has not materialised and these locomotives still present a formidable technical engineering management problem to maintain even their current relatively low availability level of 71%.'

CHAPTER 6

Class 58 — Design and Service Experience

Even before any real service experience had been built up with Class 56 certain features of the design were seen as offering scope for improvement. Some of these were introduced into later builds and have been discussed in Chapter 4; others were too radical for such an approach. It will be recalled from Chapter 1 how Class 47 evolved from prototypes which made use of monocoque body construction techniques, first adopted in the aircraft industry. This had meant that a saving in weight of around 20 tons, in comparison to the first generation Type 4s such as Classes 40, 45 and 46, had been achieved, allowing the abandonment of the 1-Co bogie configuration for the more effective Co variant. Monocoque construction required a large number of skilled metalworkers at an acceptable cost and neither factor was available in the late 1970s. In consequence Class 56 was an expensive design to build. A further problem was that interior space was limited, making maintenance difficult and air management a problem.

In 1977 BREL commissioned the BRB Design Office to produce a feasibility study for a low-cost Co-Co locomotive of around 2,500bhp for export markets. What emerged was a scheme featuring a simple load-bearing underframe, made of rolled steel joists, with lightweight superstructure which was not stressed. In 1978 the BRB decided the results of the study could form the basis for a new type of freight locomotive which would offer several advantages over Class 56, together with an anticipated 35-year life. These were: economy and ease of construction, and minimum overall maintenance costs. BREL would still be able to adapt the basic design for export markets with minimum modification. In 1979 materials procurement began for three prototypes,

which were to be evaluated in service, and, as a demonstration of faith in the new product, in January 1982 the existing order for 80 Class 56s (Lot 1510) was cut back by 35 units which would now be built as the new Class 58 (Lot 1511).

BREL Doncaster was given the contract for Lot 1511 and the second batch of 15, ordered in 1984 as Lot 1513. The underframe is the load-bearing structure of the design. Although giving the impression of being made from rolled steel joists (RSJs), in fact no RSJs or universal column of suitable dimensions could be purchased, as the relatively small quantities required for 35 plus 15 locomotives made the cost of special rolling uneconomic. Instead, the mainframe elements are made from flat plates fabricated together at Doncaster. To offer ease of machining in the Fabrication Shop a 'turnover' stand was used. For this purpose, an Asquith VNOCG gantry milling and drilling machine was acquired. (This is now in store at Crewe.) A separate turnover stand was also used in the New Erecting Shop to turn over the frames so that both sides could be machined. The frame was initially laid upside down so that the whole of the underframe equipment could be fitted, piped and wired. It was then turned over so the locomotive could be assembled over solebar level.

The frame is capable of absorbing 200-ton loads on the buffer beams, in compliance with the UIC standard. The body structure is of the 'hood' or 'bonnet' type and is divided into compartments for air management purposes. Some 32 doors, all of the same dimensions, allow access to all components and are made of pressed steel to make them easy to lift off. The equipment mounted on the underframe is assembled in modular fashion so that

Right:
Class 56 is no stranger to Deeside, having participated in the traffic flows associated with the steelworks at Shotton. When steelmaking here finished in 1980, the stockpile of iron ore was shipped to South Wales plants and this photograph is of Nos 56046 and 56033 on the 10.10 to Llanwern at Shotwick on 17 September 1980.
D. I. Rapson

Left:
Although the Type 5 fleets are concentrated on block train movements, some fill-in turns on a variety of other work can produce something unusual. After engineering activities on Sunday 4 September 1988, No 56049 was used to take a train from Westbury to Bristol East Depot. The location is just to the west of Twerton Tunnel, near Bristol. Note that the locomotive is exhibiting a trait of the class in producing a smoky exhaust. *John Chalcraft*

48

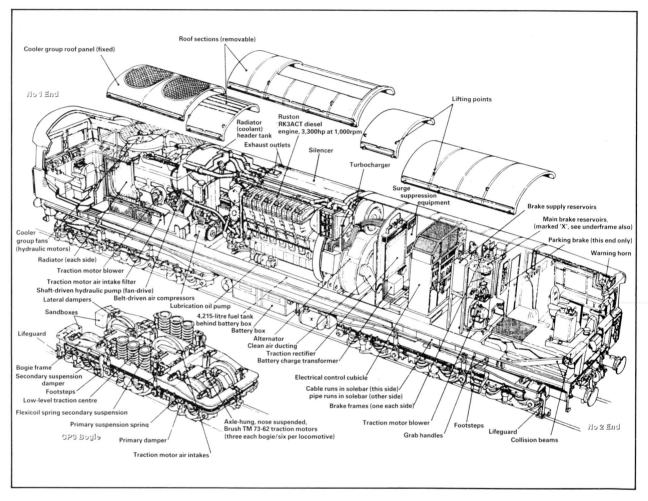

Cooler group roof panel (fixed)

Roof sections (removable)

No 1 End

Lifting points

Radiator (coolant) header tank

Ruston RK3ACT diesel engine, 3,300hp at 1,000rpm

Exhaust outlets

Silencer

Turbocharger

Surge suppression equipment

Brake supply reservoirs

Main brake reservoirs, (marked 'X', see underframe also)

Parking brake (this end only)

Warning horn

Cooler group fans (hydraulic motors)

Radiator (each side)

Traction motor blower

Traction motor air intake filter

Shaft-driven hydraulic pump (fan-drive)

Lateral dampers

Belt-driven air compressors

Sandboxes

Lubrication oil pump

4,215-litre fuel tank behind battery box

Battery box

Lifeguard

Alternator

Clean air ducting

Traction rectifier

Battery charge transformer

Bogie frame

Secondary suspension damper

Footsteps

Low-level traction centre

Flexicoil spring secondary suspension

Primary suspension spring

CP3 Bogie

Primary damper

Axle-hung, nose suspended, Brush TM 73-62 traction motors (three each bogie/six per locomotive)

Traction motor air intakes

Electrical control cubicle

Cable runs in solebar (this side) pipe runs in solebar (other side)

Brake frames (one each side)

Traction motor blower

Footsteps

Lifeguard

Grab handles

Collision beams

No 2 End

individual items can be removed with the minimum dismantling time and with a view to facilitating repair on the shop floor, rather than *in situ*, if necessary. The roof has four removable sections. A sealing plate prevents spillage on the locomotive floor dropping on to the bogies and this drains away underneath the engine.

Cab design offers a number of improvements over previous practice. Firstly, the cabs (two per locomotive) are modular and are fabricated away from the locomotive; they are then bolted on. This means they are easy to remove and repair, in the event of damage and also are sealed units to prevent draughts. The rear bulkhead is a strength structure to help prevent a cab being crushed in the event of a derailment. Having a rolled steel channel frame, a cable can be threaded along the channel to assist in rerailing. Large windows of toughened glass are provided on three sides. Access is via a single door at the rear of the cab which leads on to a walkway running across the locomotive, with another door at each end of this walkway. The rear cab door was originally of cast aluminium but from 1984 a redesigned fabricated version was adopted, being cheaper and simpler to produce. Heating can be either by using engine coolant waste heat via a heat exchanger or by means of a 2kW electric heater, if the diesel is not in use. Force ventilation by fan is available, with or without heat. A nonslip plywood floor covering is used.

Care was taken to lay out the driving controls in line with ergonomic principles. The knee-hole position was abandoned, as can be seen from Figure 5.

DSD and vigilance equipment is fitted. The class is equipped to work in multiple and can also work in multiple with Class 56. Union acceptance of the new proposals was gained before construction began; this involved the production of a wooden mock-up.

Air management within locomotives has developed considerably down the years and particular care was taken with Class 58 to get the airflow correct. The space between the two cabs is divided into four sections. Firstly, there is the cooler group and a traction motor blower. Next comes the power unit and compressors. The third section houses the turbocharger air inlet and electrical equipment. Finally, there is the electrical control equipment, main rectifier, a second traction motor blower and the brake equipment. Bulkheads are provided by the end walls of the cooler group, a flush-fit bulkhead across the carcase of the main alternator, another just clear of the free end of the main alternator,

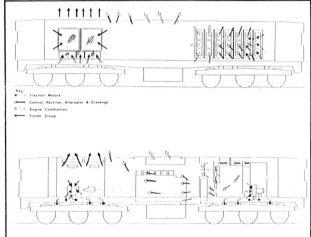

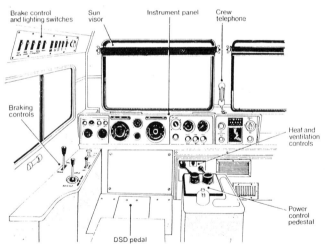

Figure 5 (far left): Class 58 Driving Position.

Figure 6 (left): Class 58: Air Management Schematic.

Instruments and switches are mounted in a console fixed to the cab front. The master controller for forward/reverse and the power handles are fitted to a pedestal located to the right of the driver's seat. On a shelf below the window to the left of the driver are the locomotive and train air brake handles. As might be expected, AWS,

on to which the main rectifier is mounted and, finally, the respective bulkheads adjacent to each cab.
Starting at No 1 end, unfiltered air is drawn in, passes over the radiator panels and expelled through the roof by the radiator fans. Air for the traction motor blower comes in through filtered intakes on either side of the cooler

50

Right:
ARC's quarries at Tytherington and Whatley despatch stone to Wolverton, as well as London. The route taken involves traversing the ex-LMS Oxford-Bletchley line. This shot, on 6 August 1988, illustrates the 07.27 ex-Whatley leaving Bicester with No 56001 *Whatley* up front. Sector livery was applied in October 1987 as part of the Railfreight relaunch. *Steve Turner*

Left:
Oil traffic from West Wales used to be diagrammed for Class 56. The profusion of exhaust smoke indicates No 56039's effort as it tackles the 1 in 75 of Ashley Down Bank, Bristol. It is heading back to Wales with empty tanks from Bridgwater.
John Chalcraft

Left:
Perhaps surprisingly, the WR seems to make more use of the class on Freightliner traffic than either the ER or LMR. The main duty is to take the Pengam-Glasgow service as far as Crewe, returning with the balancing working. The Newcastle service has also been covered by the class. This 1986 illustration, taken in evening sunlight, shows an eastbound train approaching Newport, Gwent. *M. G. Miller*

group module and passes over the compressor intercooler and aftercooler before being directed on to the motors on No 1 bogie. Apart from small inlets for the two air compressors, the engine room is sealed against the ingress of air from the outside. A filtered supply for cooling and combustion is received via the main alternator. The side panels behind the alternator bulkhead contain filters and air is drawn through them for engine combustion and the turbochargers. Filtered air is also drawn into the clean air compartment at No 2 end to cool the brake and electrical control gear, the main rectifier and for use by the traction motor blower serving No 2 bogie. It exhausts to the engine compartment.

For Class 58 the same main electrical components as fitted to Class 56 have been specified as these have worked satisfactorily. Ruston was able to offer its RK diesel in 12-cylinder Mk 3a form, following further improvements, and this had been giving excellent service in No 47901. Set to deliver 3,300bhp at 1,000rpm, those fitted to Class 58 have a single turbocharger, unlike that in No 47901, which has two; this gives a saving in maintenance. Further advantages of the 12RK3ACT over its 16-cylinder predecessor are that it is more fuel-efficient, with savings of 5-6%, whilst the provision of four fewer cylinders gives a reduced initial cost. Unlike the 16RK3CT Mk 3, the air inlet manifold is not incorporated into the centre of the crankcase and the leakage problems of the bellows, joints and clamps which bedevil Class 56 have been minimised by reducing the number of components in the exhaust system from 28 to only 10 in Class 58. Among other benefits, the space it formerly occupied can be used for a larger, more efficient silencer to meet UIC limits. Whereas on Class 56 the silencer is roof-mounted, in Class 58 it is bolted to the engine. This allows the roof to be removed more easily, and to be of lighter construction, and also means the problems of the flexible connections between engine and silencer are overcome. Finally, having only 12 cylinders, the engine takes up less space.

As expected, the Brush ac power generation equipment installed in Class 56 is used, the main alternator being a Brush BA1101B and the auxiliary alternator a BAA602B. Equally, the same traction motors as those fitted to Class 56 are employed, permitting interchangeability between the classes. For normal operation the motors are connected in series-parallel and have a single stage of field weakening. Motor pairings are 1+6, 2+5 and 4+3, different to Class 56 which is configured 1+2, 3+4 and 5+6. With a view to counteracting wheelslip due to weight transfer during starting, one motor in each pairing was connected permanently in weak field, the motor in question being determined by the direction of travel. A current balance system of wheelslip detection was fitted to the first few but this was revised based on early experience; more details are given later. Operation in slow-speed mode could be at one of three speeds, as for Class 56; the speeds are 0.5, 1 and 2.7mph. A fourth setting is provided for starting a heavy train under poor adhesion conditions and sets a limit on the tractive effort. Whilst in slow-speed mode engine speed remains at idling, with main alternator excitation controlled by the slow-speed unit and load regulator. In this mode the traction motors are connected in series. A design feature is that the voltage is fixed slightly higher than would ordinarily be required to induce a slight amount of slipping. This is to cope with rail debris and also prevent all tractive effort being removed (as would happen with Class 56 with its traction motors in series-parallel) if slipping occurred due to poor adhesion. By having a voltage limiting circuit it was intended that wheel speed would be limited if an axle went into slip.

As with much of the other equipment, the cooler group is a separate module. Its main housing is of BREL manufacture and houses the radiator components supplied by the manufacturer specified. In line with BR sourcing policy, equipment from two manufacturers was specified, Serck and Covrad. The former uses individual elements, the latter cooling panels; Serck is slightly more expensive. Both systems make use of hydrostatic radiator fan drive, with the hydrostatic pump being driven off the free end of the engine. For Nos 58001-4/15-30/32-5 Serck was specified, for Nos 58005-14 Covrad/Commercial Shearing specified. In service it has been found that the Covrad panels are very difficult to keep watertight, those of Serck manufacture less so. Hydrostatic drive has the advantage of giving infinitely variable control but in BR service, hydrostatic systems have proved difficult to keep leaktight. Past experience with EE diesels fitted with mechanical radiator fan drive had established the success of the system, except for overcooling in winter. Mechanical drive involves a power take-off from the free end of the engine driving the radiator fan directly. Such a system was tried in No 58031, incorporating a thermostatically controlled clutch to avoid overcooling the engine, and the last 15 locomotives have been similarly equipped. Covrad panels are used. Apart from being free of leaks, mechanical drive involves less maintenance.

Two separate circuits exist within the cooler group. A primary circuit absorbs heat from the diesel engine coolant, with a dissipation rate of 631.5kW. The secondary circuit, with a dissipation rate of 756.4kW, cools the intercooler and the lubricating oil heat exchanger. Based on experience with Class 56, a header tank with a much larger capacity is fitted.

The PBL brake control system is less complicated than other systems. From the driver's point of view, the amount of brake application is determined not by the angle of turn of the brake valve but by the time the valve is held in the 'apply' position. The brake pipe pressure control unit is a variation of the Davies & Metcalfe E70 unit used in Class 56. As part of the redesign of the cab layout, the driver's brake controls are of the joystick type, with forward movement giving application and rearward movement giving release. For emergency applications a push button is provided which vents the brake pipe direct to atmosphere.

Although the CP1 bogie, fitted under No 56042, had been designed for long service life and minimal maintenance, a change was necessary for Class 58; this was due to the different superstructure layout. In addition, the solid underframe of the new class would not flex to the same extent as that of a Class 56. The new CP3 bogie is also a mixture of castings and fabricated sections. Sandboxes were initially only fitted on the outer faces of the bogie and sanding was both automatic and under driver-control. Early service experience, though, highlighted two problems. Firstly, inadequate sanding of the rear bogie became evident and was solved by fitting sandboxes to the inner face of each bogie. This led to a revision in the brake gear to accommodate the new boxes and caused a change from Westinghouse to SAB equipment. No 58020 was modified experimentally and then all new builds from No 58036 included the redesign, designated CP3a. Secondly, on uneven track equalisation of the axles on a bogie was insufficient and gave rise to poor adhesion. This was solved by softening the primary springs on the middle axle of each bogie. A study was carried out in 1983 to assess the CP3 but, as no more of the class are envisaged, its findings are unlikely to be taken further to any great extent. In any event, the objective of producing a bogie which will run for eight to 10 years between shopping, seems to have been achieved.

A considerable amount of research was made by BREL Doncaster into the constructional practices used in other industries. This reflected in some of the assembly procedures adopted, though others, such as snap-in connections for electrical components, were rejected by BRB Derby. The decision to have a slimmed-in bodyside between the cabs was said to be following American 'hood unit' practice with a view to winning export orders. Another explanation was that it served to keep traincrews out of the engine room so they could not touch equipment. This feature has backfired, for the very narrow external walkway has led to the imposition of a regulation that equipment inside the locomotive hood can only be worked on when alongside staging. Further, as the engine overspeed trip switch is inside the hood, it means an engine shutdown due to this cause cannot now be reset by the driver and the locomotive becomes a failure.

Work on No 58001 got underway in mid-February 1981 when the first plate was cut. When the first frame had been fabricated it was sent to Davy Leorvy of Sheffield on 27 August 1981; this was done for the first three examples as the Asquith milling and drilling machine had not been installed. It was returned on 18 September and laid in the New Erecting Shop for fitting out to begin. After machining, the frames for No 58003 went from Sheffield to the Railway Technical Centre for extensive stress analysis tests.

Right:
**During the 1980s Type 5s
have penetrated into SR
territory from two main
directions, from the LMR
via the West London line
and from the WR, mainly
from Westbury. Although
the stone traffic out of
Merehead quarry is now
in the care of Class 59,
ARC still relies on
Class 56 motive power.
No 56052 crosses the
Portsmouth line at
Woking, transferring
stone hoppers between
the up and down yards on
24 May 1985.**
Colin Grafham

Left:
When Doncaster had responsibility for works repair up to 1986 it sent an outshopped machine for a light, high-speed trip along the East Coast main line. Crewe, however, usually attached a locomotive to the front of a Euston-Holyhead working forward from Crewe. On 20 May 1987 No 56090 had obviously performed satisfactorily as it has made a return trip down the North Wales main line. It is seen piloting No 47439 on the 13.00 Holyhead-Euston entering Crewe. The Class 56 has received the revised Railfreight grey scheme, which included the solebar being painted red. *D. I. Rapson*

No particular problems were encountered during construction and a good rate of production was achieved. During 1985, 15 units were turned out and this rate continued in 1986. The last of the class, No 58050, was selected to be fitted with some of Brush's SEPEX equipment. SEPEX involves the separate excitation of the traction motor field coils and is with a view to giving better adhesion. No 58050 was actually built as a conventional machine but then fitted with a modified alternator and control cubicle. The delay in delivery of the latter caused a protracted stay in works before No 58050 made its debut. As this delay was outside BREL's control, it was handed over to the Director of Mechanical & Electrical Engineering before the cubicle had been fitted. It retained standard traction motors, to give uniformity with the rest of the class, but had speed sensing on each motor and a groundspeed radar is installed to measure trackspeed precisely. Another piece of detail which made it unusual was that it was fitted with a 'used' diesel engine which had already seen service in another Class 58. Three spare power units had been bought and all had been needed to replace failures in earlier class members before No 58050 was built. Although such warranty repairs were normally carried out by Ruston at its Vulcan factory, as No 58050 needed a specially mounted alternator, the engine it received had the repair work done at Doncaster.

It is understood that the SEPEX equipment functioned very well and has, no doubt, contributed towards Brush winning the Class 60 order, as will be described in a later chapter. In mid-1988 a major failure brought the decision to convert No 58050 to a standard Class 58 and this was done at BRML Doncaster. It seems that during its short life whilst SEPEX-fitted it did little revenue-earning work and was more of a development machine for Brush.

A new livery was adopted which represented the first of the new Sector colour schemes. All-yellow cabs had large black numbers under the driver's side windows whilst a 'RAILFREIGHT' transfer was fixed to the opposite side cab panel; the cab windows were outlined in black. Bodysides were in Railfreight grey and contained the BR emblem in the middle. The large solebar was painted red and the overall effect was quite striking. The narrow body profile has been commented on above; it meant that running the locomotives through a washing plant did not clean the side panels. In the autumn of 1987 Railfreight changed this livery to two-tone grey, as noted in the chapter dealing with Class 56. For display at the launch of the new colour scheme at Ripple Lane in October of that year, No 58050 was repainted in this style. At the handing-over ceremony of No 58001 on 9 December 1982, it was formally named *Railfreight* though a proper nameplate was not carried. Whilst details of names carried are to be found at the end of this book, a slight curiosity surrounds the plates carried by No 58020. This was originally named *Doncaster Works BRE* and the background to the 'BRE' part of the plates painted in blue. Later new plates were cast which omitted the 'BRE' suffix.

As with any new class of locomotive, experience in daily use brought to light certain areas where modifications were desirable. The 12RK3ACT diesel engine had been running very successfully in No 47901 since early 1981. Some concern was expressed at first in Class 58 over the very low oil consumption in comparison to the 16K3CT version in Class 56. It was eventually decided that this was just a good feature and nothing to worry about. In cold weather the diesel engine was often difficult to start. One option considered was the fitting of an ether cold start, but a slight retardation of the timing of the engine overcame the problem. Far more worrying was a spate of piston fractures. What was perplexing for the Ruston engineers was that No 47901 was not experiencing similar problems, particularly as it was then still set to deliver 3,500bhp, as opposed to the 3,300bhp rating for the engines in Class 58. It was to enable a more detailed examination of the pistons in the Class 47 to be made that it was taken to Toton in May 1986 and a replacement set of pistons fitted. Although there were signs of deterioration, put down to being run at the higher rating, the original pistons were otherwise satisfactory. The Class 58 experiences were blamed on the piston manufacturer and a campaign change put in hand. It was at this time that the timing was retarded slightly to give easier cold starting.

The cold weather also caused freezing in the braking system during extreme conditions. Residual water or moisture in the reduction valve would freeze when a straight air brake application was made, due to the cooling effect of the flow of air. Pipe lagging and shielding had no significant effect and in the end a modification was fitted which bypassed the reduction valve to give a 10 bar application to the cab air network.

Whereas there was much satisfaction in the refinements which enabled a very fuel-efficient diesel engine to be produced, with only a single turbocharger, during tests on the road it was found that under part load turbocharger surging was taking place. Whilst surging under full power has been a problem on, among others, Class 56, there has been no parallel experience on BR of this happening at part load. Ruston was able to remedy the situation but only at the expense of high turbine inlet temperatures which are also undesirable. For the time being, though, these have been accepted and, indeed, are no higher than apply on Class 56. Although the two manufacturers of the silencer each confirmed their products would meet the UIC requirement for 100dbA at 1m distance, in fact neither achieved this in service. A revised silencer box, needing a larger space, was eventually produced and fitted from No 58027 onwards. Research in conjunction with Southampton University has also taken place and, to date, five different designs of silencer have been fitted.

Fuel dilution has affected BR's diesel fleet for many years. It is generally understood to be caused, in part, by a diesel 'running cold', due to, say, idling for long periods in cold weather. With the cold start difficulties of Class 58 there was a need to leave the engines idling for long periods and engine oil changes after only 300hr to 400hr were found to be necessary. What was again puzzling was that No 47901 was not affected. It has the Class 56 type of secondary cooling circuit which gives higher charge air cooling temperatures. In their early days Class 56 locomotives were more prone to fuel dilution than became the case in later years, and there is the possibility that, with Class 58, it will prove to be a running-in problem. A revised fuel injector, which is at present under design, could provide a solution.

Wheelslip detection at first used a current balance system. During the early trials with No 58001 it was found that the system was not correcting wheelslip adequately. At first the current balance comparator was improved to match more closely the traction motor characteristic but still the system's performance failed to match that used in Class 56. Eventually the Class 56 voltage balance system was fitted retrospectively to all examples. Until the change had been made the class was not accepted for traffic and this explains why Nos 58001-9 were all taken into LMR stock on 28 February 1984. The modification to soften the bogie middle axle primary springing has already been mentioned. Tests on the Railway Technical Centre weighbridge showed a 25% improvement but overall performance was still inferior to Class 56. Service trials were carried out during 1985 when No 58004, with modified springing, and No 58005, with standard arrangement, were evaluated at Sutton colliery with Test Car 6. In practice, the revised springing failed to offer a significant improvement in performance where track and adhesion conditions were poor. Further consideration of the problem has also highlighted the dangers of railburn due to wheelslip whilst operating in slow-speed mode with the traction motors in series. Here it was found that axle speeds of up to 20mph were taking place, instead of the specified 0.5mph for the locomotive. The Class 56 slow-speed arrangement, which keeps the traction motors in series-parallel, was better and it is understood that No 58008 has been modified to this pattern.

As conceived, the Class 58 was to be rugged, simple and deliver a high tractive effort, even under poor rail conditions. It was hoped to be a basis for BREL to compete in foreign markets and be the flagship of the Railfreight fleet, being multiplied to 200 units, but this has not been the case.

What has been achieved with Class 58 is a product which took 20% less time to build and at 15% less cost than Class 56, which is also cheaper and easier to run than the latter class and which has won the approval of depot staff for its ease of maintenance.

Right:
Construction of Class 58 was undertaken entirely at Doncaster. The interior of the Doncaster Works Class 58 erecting shop on 25 November 1985 finds Nos 58037/8/6 in various stages of completion, whilst a Class 56 receives an Intermediate repair in the background. Note that the frames of No 58038 are inverted for fitting out of underside equipment, which was normal practice.
David N. Clough

Left:
Class 58 was designed to be a better prime mover than Class 56. The importance of CEGB coal traffic to BR is such that the fleet was, from new, put on to MGR diagrams, replacing the older Type 5. Hence Trent Valley power stations witness much of their activity. Toton is the location for this August 1985 view of No 58022, which is in charge of 7N50, 17.09 Ratcliffe-on-Soar CEGB-Bentinck NCB. *D. I. Rapson*

CHAPTER 7

Class 58 — Allocation and Utilisation

As this class has been diagrammed almost exclusively on MGR coal traffic, there is not a great deal of variety to discuss. From new, all the fleet has always been allocated to Toton Traction Depot, once accepted into revenue-earning service. This is not to say that all its work has been off that depot, for, with increasing numbers in service, examples have worked off a number of crew signing-on points; notable in this respect are Bescot, Coalville and Saltley on the LMR and Barrow Hill and Shirebrook on the ER. How the class spread over the period 1984 to 1988 will become evident later.

Firstly, though, it is worth charting the early period of construction and commissioning. The first metal plate for use in No 58001 was cut in mid-February 1981. The plan, at this time, was for three prototypes to run in service before a larger order was placed, to allow any teething troubles to be ironed out on a few, rather than a large number of locomotives. During 1982, though, an order was placed for a further 32, straight off the drawing board, as it were, and so this original plan was not seen through. In view of some of the modifications which were needed before the class was accepted into traffic, this was unfortunate and demonstrated, yet again, that BR never learns the lesson of plunging headlong into new designs.

By late November 1982 No 58001 was undergoing load bank tests in Doncaster works but was, of course, ready (superficially at least) to be handed over to Railfreight at the ceremony on the works on 9 December. No 58001 did not emerge on to the main line for over three months and it seems its first trial trip was on 21 March 1983 when it took eight Mk 2 coaches to Peterborough. Not being fitted with vacuum brake equipment it could not haul the standard Doncaster test rake. Ten days later it was undergoing a heavy load trial with a rake of MGRs on the Lincoln line. Meanwhile the diesel engine from No 58002 had apparently been returned to Ruston. On 28 April No 58001 broke new ground when it hauled 6D68 from Doncaster Decoy to Immingham Coal Terminal. During May No 58001 was undergoing trials in the Doncaster and Sheffield areas whilst No 58002 had moved to Toton for crew training, having run on trial to Peterborough on 12 May.

On 14 July No 58002 worked a Toton-Willesden freight throughout as no electric locomotive was available at Northampton to replace it. A summary of the position on the works on 11 September was as follows: No 58005 complete in primer, No 58006 on test, No 58007 complete and part painted, Nos 58008-14 under construction. The honour of the first passenger duty fell to No 58002 on 18 September when it worked a charter from Nuneaton to Matlock. As part of continuing trials No 58001 worked over from Derby to Crewe and penetrated down the West Coast main line as far as Winsford on the 26th before returning to Derby. October marked the beginning of the class's association with the Ratcliffe power station-Fletton fly ash services, both Nos 58002/4 being recorded.

By the end of November all the class up to No 58009 had made trial runs to Peterborough; by now these were made light engine. On 9 November No 58004 assisted failed No 56059 on the Cliffe Hill-Hayes and Harlington Tarmac train whilst on 22 November No 58002 made the inaugural run for the class to Merseyside with a coal train for Garston Dock. Haulage of the Tarmac train up the Midland main line was repeated on 1 December, this time with No 58005 piloting No 56061. Before 1983 ended Class 58 locomotives were at work in the Coalville area.

In February 1984 Nos 58005/6 were noted at Saltley and Bescot respectively for crew training. On 8 February Nos 58009/2 were at King's Norton on a car train. No 58002 took over crew training duties at Saltley later in February and had the honour of taking the first Class 58-powered MGR to Didcot, originating from Kingsbury, on 29 February. Fitting for driver-only operation (DOO) was done retrospectively to all those built so far in early 1984 and incorporated from new with the rest. Westhouses was receiving visits by March and by this date deliveries to Toton had reached No 58014. This locomotive was soon despatched to Reading for driver training, as men from that depot relieve incoming crews arriving at Didcot power station. The miners' strike cut down the demand for the class and specials were run over a number of routes for training purposes; one such was, surprisingly, from Droitwich to Worcester. During the same period examples were used to haul Bescot-Willesden freights. The first scheduled passenger train was covered on 1 April when No 58004 took a diverted Birmingham-Euston service as far as Nuneaton. Such Class 1 duties have continued intermittently ever since.

Although work on Freightliners had not, so far, amounted to more than a small proportion of total mileage, on 10 June No 58012 took charge of a Bescot to Banbury trip. On the 30th No 58011 had charge of the 12.20 SO Lawley Street-Southampton liner and No 58002 did the same trip seven days later. Return visits to works were not uncommon, either for rectification or modification. In addition to the high-speed test run the same sort of slow-speed trial on MGR stock as had been used for new Class 56s brought visits to the Scunthorpe area. Meanwhile on 20 June No 58008 had undergone trials down the branch to Runcorn Folly Lane, having travelled down from Bescot. No 58012 made an appearance at Bristol on 9 July hauling a 'dead' Class 47. By now, construction of No 58025 was underway and the first 35 were expected to be in service by the end of 1985.

Appearances on passenger trains began to become more frequent as the fleet size and distribution rose. On 1 September No 58002 was summoned from Saltley to tow a failed IC125 unit, forming the 12.10 Liverpool-Penzance, forward from Birmingham. Surprisingly, the procession continued to Plymouth, where the train was terminated, the Class 58 being a failure with flat batteries. This problem, common at the time, has been described elsewhere. A week later No 58007 turned up at Sheffield on a relief from Poole whilst on 6 December No 58008 was removed from a Bescot-Oxford Speedlink to assist failed Class 47 No 47432 on the 05.50 Paddington-Liverpool forward from Banbury. Back on 26 September No 58010 made its way via Springs Branch to Southport for display at an Open Day. As 1984 drew to a close No 58020 made its trial run to Peterborough whilst No 58031 was being assembled in the works.

More new ground was broken on 29 April 1985 when No 58028, then ex-works, reached Tyneside on a rake of MGRs. The following week the first recorded triple-header passed Saltley, Nos 58026/23/25 being involved. Supply problems with radiators caused No 58007 to be out of service for nearly 12 months. It arrived at Doncaster on 13 November 1984 and, together with No 58008, had to wait for Covrad to come up with the necessary components. In due course it was decided to fit No 58008 with the spare Serck cooler group (both types being specified, see Chapter 6) whilst the replacement parts for No 58007 were fitted instead into No 58006, which had also suffered a similar failure. Finally a modified cooler group was used to get No 58007 back to work.

Further crew training, this time of Speke drivers, found No 58016 en route from Toton on 9 June; this would then allow Toton drivers to be relieved whilst their trains were taken through Garston Dock. It is interesting to note that the training involved at least one run along the North Wales coast to Llandudno. Next month No 58019 had taken over at Speke and the same trip was made on a weekly basis. More profitable work included use on 12 June on the 17.40 Seaforth-Garston Freightliner and on 4 August it took the 11.10 ecs out of Lime Street to Edge Hill carriage sidings. Crew training at the depot was completed on 18 October and by the end of the month all of the 33 units so far in traffic had appeared at Garston. On 22 July No 58022 tackled the 12.45 Curzon Street-

Right:
With the closure of the Woodhead route, export coal from the East Midlands was transferred to the Hope Valley and then routed instead via Stoke-on-Trent and down the West Coast main line from Crewe. By this time, Class 58s were taking a hand in its shipment, with Garston crews having been trained on them. On 23 April 1987, No 58018 takes 6F24 export coal from Toton to Garston through Crewe.
D. I. Rapson

Left:
In the same way that Class 56 had done before, Class 58 soon began to appear on the Fletton fly ash service. Approaching Stamford, work-stained No 58029 provided the motive power for the working from Ratcliffe power station on 20 August 1987.
Graham Hudson

Penyffordd. This was not an isolated instance, as several other members of the class were utilised before Class 56 again took over.

Diversions on 1 December caused by electric locomotive No 86225 losing its pantograph near Berkswell, and the consequent overhead line problems, brought Nos 58003/12/32 into passenger service between Nuneaton and Birmingham. At the time the class put in numerous visits to Tyseley for various modifications, including changing of pistons, to be carried out. Leaving aside the exhibition of No 58021 at Stewarts Lane Open Day in September 1985, No 58010 seems to have been the first to do any work on the SR's Eastern Division. Probably as a result of a change in diagramming the 09.12 Silverhill-Northfleet and 23.00 Northfleet-Toton began to see regular Class 58 coverage from January 1986; No 58010 was actually seen on 9 January. The last day of the month found No 58033 in strange territory undertaking a strange duty; it departed Old Oak Common depot towing Nos 47425/31287/45143/47365 back to Saltley.

Associated with the fracturing of pistons, No 58005 was back at Doncaster works during February for load bank testing; Toton's load bank had been burnt out by a Class 59. June saw two unusual pieces of Class 1 activity. First, on the 7th, No 58037 set off from Birmingham for Reading with the 05.53 Bradford-Poole, returning with the 11.40 Poole-Liverpool throughout; finally it returned to Birmingham with the 19.05 Paddington service. Five days later it was No 58033's turn when it took over the 07.26 Taunton-Inverness at New Street and proceeded as far as Crewe. The allocation of locomotives to sub-Sectors in November meant all the class was allocated for trainload coal use. Summer 1986 found crew training in progress at Shirebrook, with Class 58 being diagrammed off that depot from the winter timetable; although Worksop men do not know the type. During 1987 the pattern of work settled down very much in line with this framework. Appearance on other freight and emergency passenger activity is not unknown but there is far less mileage put in at present on air braked service (ABS) freights than was the case in 1984/85.

Obviously the teething problems of a new design can cause downward fluctuations in its performance. Figure 7 reproduces details of availability and miles per casualty for the first two years of revenue-earning service.

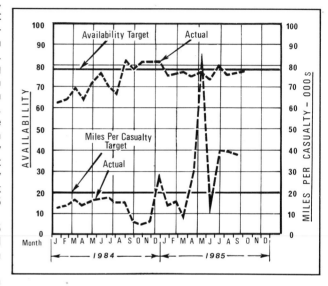

By 1988 matters had settled down and availability was generally in the mid to high 80s as a percentage of the total fleet. The first of the class have undergone F exams and overall performance can be considered as meeting expectations. Indeed the only facet which leaves the class markedly inferior to Class 59 is in starting ability. Who knows, in the next decade, when the class comes up for mid-life re-engineering, this difference may be removed.

CHAPTER 8
Class 59 — Design and Utilisation

Whilst BR is run on commercial lines it seems it took the impetus from a third party to bring some creative new thinking into Railfreight operating practices. In the days of steam it was recognised that regular manning of a locomotive by two sets of traincrew was conducive to achieving better performance in terms of timekeeping and reduced maintenance, as opposed to the common user principle. Modern traction is more economical to run than steam because its 'down-time' for daily servicing is markedly less and it can operate for longer periods than a driver's turn of duty. This rules out regular manning practices; it also brings the disadvantages of 'common user' operation.

Foster Yeoman Ltd (FY) is a privately-owned quarrying company, whose main extraction site is currently Merehead quarry in East Somerset. Of the 1983 level of output of over 3 million tons of stone, some 75% was shipped by rail to a number of terminals in Southeast England. FY already operated its own wagon fleet under a leasing and maintenance agreement with Procor and had facilities at Merehead for the fleet to be maintained. High utilisation was obtained, just in the same way that any successful road haulier does likewise with his lorry fleet. By contrast, however, BR's operating policy and practice had centred round the use of an availability definition which does not usually secure peak utilisation.

For diagramming purposes, the number of loco-motives available for traffic at 06.00 each day is the important factor. Design factors influence the reliability and, as a result, the availability of different classes, as also does the ease of maintenance and availability of spares. Apart from IC125 sets, generally BR's diesel locomotive fleet is rostered on the basis that 70-75% (depending on the class) of the fleet will be available for service use, whether or not there are any services to run. Routine and unscheduled maintenance is carried out primarily on a two/three-shift, five/six/seven-day week

basis, depending on the depot concerned. The larger ones operate 24hr days, seven days a week, smaller ones may only work a five or six-day week, with just two shifts.

This approach does not, however, square with operating needs for traffic purposes. Passenger flows peak at morning and evening rush hour and are at a minimum during the night. With mail trains the demand is almost entirely nocturnal. Freight, though, is more complex; different customers want their goods shipped to suit their particular requirements. Whilst BR takes account of such factors when diagramming motive power, the competing aim of a steady throughput at depots means that rarely can both be met. Generally the upshot has been a locomotive fleet which is bigger than it might be, which is therefore more costly than it could be and which results in the customers paying more than they need to. With a fleet of 135, Class 56 represents an investment at cost to BR of about £135 million. Assuming three-quarters of the locomotives can be rostered regularly, this means that about £34 million worth of locomotives have to stand idle under repair at any one time. Put another way, for every three Class 56s hired by a customer to transport his cargo, he has to pay for a fourth locomotive to be on a depot. Find a road haulage contractor who only has two-thirds of his wagons at work and you will find one close to going broke. It is therefore easy to see why Railfreight is uncompetitive.

There is nothing ingenious about the above analysis; it is just commercial commonsense. It was therefore not surprising that in 1983 FY sought a better deal from BR in terms of the prime movers provided to haul the stone traffic. Having witnessed a steady stream of different locomotives of the same class, by then Class 56, turning up each day at Merehead, and having had to suffer delays in delivery and disruption to wagon rostering due to the high failure rate of these locomotives, FY asked for a dedicated fleet of six of the class for its traffic. As an

Right:
No 58050 *Toton Traction Depot* returns an empty MGR to the south Derbyshire coalfield from Willington CEGB. It is seen at Claymills near Burton-on-Trent on 6 October 1988.
A. O. Wynn

Left:
Didcot power station receives fuel from a number of East and West Midlands collieries. Some of these use the main line south of Birmingham as far as Coventry. This shot illustrates No 58031 at Berkswell on 31 August 1987. *Steve Turner*

alternative to this little sub-fleet being maintained at Bristol Bath Road, FY suggested maintenance be carried out at enlarged facilities at Merehead. By rescheduling trains out of the quarry it would be possible for all the output to be handled by just six units, which could be maintained during periods when they would not be required, principally at weekends. Such an arrangement would enable 95% of the booked trains to be covered by this sub-fleet, without the need to keep an additional three Class 56s standing idle, if the usual 70% availability target was followed. The result could be lower costs to both BR and FY.

It is outside the scope of this book to discuss further how the concept of dedicated fleets has since evolved on other parts of the BR network with apparent success. The idea of high availability is only one which has now been taken on board in specifying the next generation of freight motive power, as will be seen in the final chapter.

Detailed consideration by both Railfreight and FY of the financial implications of the ideas outlined above drew the conclusion that FY would be in an even better position if it owned its own fleet. Accordingly, in early December 1983 the Mechanical & Electrical Engineering, Operating and Employee Relations Departments of BR came on the scene to consider the feasibility of the use of privately-owned diesels in daily service on the system. Although this was not a new concept — HS4000 *Kestrel* was a private-owner vehicle — industrial relations attitudes had changed. In the past the likes of *Kestrel* were British products; set against a backdrop of redundancies at BREL workshops, there was the possibility of FY meeting its needs from abroad. It has been suggested that the BRB was keen to evaluate some features included in overseas designs and FY presented them with an excellent opportunity to do so.

High productivity from the new fleet was sensible commercially; the same principle already applied to the FY wagon fleet. It did not involve much recasting of the stone train movements to build in sufficient turnround time at Merehead to permit routine inspection and fuelling of the locomotives on a daily basis, with maintenance concentrated at weekends. To adhere to diagrams, though, would involve, technically, 100%

availability, on a revised definition of number of actual turns worked divided by number of turns booked, multiplied by 100. To allow for a contingency margin to cover for the unexpected, FY, in seeking quotes from interested manufacturers, stipulated a guaranteed 95% availability, with proof from existing usage that this could be attained. No British manufacturer could offer this and so FY turned to General Motors (GM) of America, in particular its Electro-Motive Division (EMD), which had supplied a shunting locomotive for use in the Merehead quarry.

Although full details of the business specification have not been released, it can be gleaned that, in addition to 95% booked turn availability, a Co-Co, twin-cab design of around 3,000-3,500bhp was sought, with an axle loading no greater than 21.5 tonnes. FY was seeking six units, this being based on how many Class 56 diesels were needed to move the trains, some of which required two of the class in multiple, as they grossed 4,300 tonnes. This need for multiple working was due to limitations in the capability of a Class 56 to start a train. When GM-EMD looked at the performance specification it felt that one of its SD50 diesel-electrics, fitted with the patented Super Series high adhesion facility, could handle the trains then booked for two Class 56s. Use of a single GM diesel on a train of 4,380 tonnes was calculated as adding 30min to a round trip time of 195min from Westbury to Acton and back; this was considered acceptable.

Super Series (SS) is a system developed during the 1970s and first applied in 1978 in America in response to that country's railways demands for greater haulage capacity but without the disadvantages of higher capital, fuel and maintenance costs associated with higher horsepower. It utilises wheelcreep or controlled slipping to increase friction at the wheelrim and so provide better adhesion. A full description of the system was given to the Institution of Mechanical Engineers Conference at York in April 1987 by its designer, B. R. Meyer and subsequently published. It operates only at low speed, when adhesion factors tend to be more critical, and relies on a groundspeed radar to measure precisely true speed. To produce extra adhesion, the control system produces, at any given speed, a degree of wheelcreep, the wheels turning slightly faster than true speed in a form of rail controlled slip, and this achieves the desired result, plus reducing sand consumption and hence cutting rail and tyre wear.

By specifying SS-fitted locomotives FY was thus able to cut about one-third off the capital cost of its fleet, providing still further savings. Agreement was reached between FY and GM for the purchase of four EMD JT26CW-SS (J is two-cab, T turbocharged, 26 denotes 16 cylinders, CW means two six-wheel bogies) diesel-electrics, based on the SD40-2 type, with BR exercising a right of control over aspects of the design to conform with British practice, and contracts were signed on 29 November 1984.

For GM it was not just a simple translation of an existing product to meet local needs. The British loading gauge meant a scaling-down of the SD40, whilst the need to include engine silencing to meet EEC noise emission levels was not normal practice. Health and Safety legislation caused a reconfiguration of the control cubicle to segregate high and low voltage systems whilst BR wished all future cabs to be based on that conceived for Class 58, being modular and with instruments and controls in the usual positions. Another feature copied from Class 58 was the Westinghouse PBL brake system but the narrow body of the British design was not emulated. Whilst this feature had been copied in Class 58 from American practice, as seen in Chapter 6 it had not proved practicable in Britain, so the new FY diesels, designated Class 59, featured a full-width body, but with roof hatches and modular assembly to make removal of components as easy as possible. This meant a structural underframe was to be used, rather than having stressed skin bodysides which could be load bearing.

To attain high adhesion the GM HT-C bogie was incorporated and its massive size dominates the locomotive. Gauge problems brought a change in brake rigging, with Class 58-type SAB brake cylinders being fitted. Coupled with the strength underframe, the car body (to use American parlance) appears to sit very high off the ground, a distinctive feature of the class. Manual sanding is available up to 5mph, GM's 16 645-EC diesel

was installed, rated at 3,300bhp at 904rpm. This two-stroke machine has a long history of use in rail traction applications but a curious feature is the need to keep the turbocharger oil feed circulating for 15-20min after the engine has been shut down, something of a weak spot, for, if the pump does not remain running after shutdown, then the diesel must be restarted. It is interesting to note that, whilst the GM diesel has attracted much praise, in the 1960s Sulzer, in developing its LVA range, rejected a two-stroke cycle in favour of a four-stroke, having carried out extensive tests of both. A two-stroke, though, is said to be quicker to control during wheelslip correction. In order to install silencers of sufficient size to meet UIC specifications, the space which they occupy resulted in the abandonment of dynamic brake equipment. In an SD40 the resistance banks which dissipate the heat generated by the braking effort are mounted in the roof, but in Class 59 room was not available for their accommodation.

Power generation is by a main alternator group (Model AR11MLD-D14A) and companion alternator group (Model D14A), both with rectifiers. Whilst the main alternator maximum current is 7,020A, it has not been possible to ascertain the continuous rating, though the locomotive is rated at 3,000 traction hp. Six Model D77B traction motors are employed, rated continuously at 900A, 720hp. Such a high rating suggests a standard motor in the GM range, certainly well above Class 59 requirements and so well able to absorb high starting currents. The motors are connected in all-parallel across the main rectifier.

Space does not permit a full description of all the features of the design and so only the main ones have been covered above. One other aspect is worthy of mention, the primary air filtration system. This is achieved by the inertia system, using bodyside inertia filter tubes of the 'swirl', rather than 'maze' type. This feature seems to have been ignored by most writers but is of considerable interest in view of the comments made about the system fitted originally to Class 50. No data has been found to show the minimum sized particles the filters can extract. Apart from routine inspection, the system is essentially maintenance free.

**Figure 8: Class 59
General Arrangement**

INTERNAL FEATURES

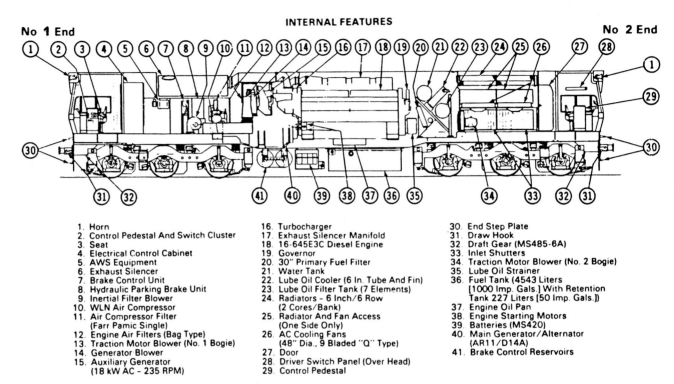

1. Horn
2. Control Pedestal And Switch Cluster
3. Seat
4. Electrical Control Cabinet
5. AWS Equipment
6. Exhaust Silencer
7. Brake Control Unit
8. Hydraulic Parking Brake Unit
9. Inertial Filter Blower
10. WLN Air Compressor
11. Air Compressor Filter
    (Farr Pamic Single)
12. Engine Air Filters (Bag Type)
13. Traction Motor Blower (No. 1 Bogie)
14. Generator Blower
15. Auxiliary Generator
    (18 kW AC - 235 RPM)

16. Turbocharger
17. Exhaust Silencer Manifold
18. 16-645E3C Diesel Engine
19. Governor
20. 30" Primary Fuel Filter
21. Water Tank
22. Lube Oil Cooler (6 In. Tube And Fin)
23. Lube Oil Filter Tank (7 Elements)
24. Radiators - 6 Inch/6 Row
    (2 Cores/Bank)
25. Radiator And Fan Access
    (One Side Only)
26. AC Cooling Fans
    (48" Dia., 9 Bladed "Q" Type)
27. Door
28. Driver Switch Panel (Over Head)
29. Control Pedestal

30. End Step Plate
31. Draw Hook
32. Draft Gear (MS485-6A)
33. Inlet Shutters
34. Traction Motor Blower (No. 2 Bogie)
35. Lube Oil Strainer
36. Fuel Tank (4543 Liters
    [1000 Imp. Gals.] With Retention
    Tank 227 Liters [50 Imp. Gals.])
37. Engine Oil Pan
38. Engine Starting Motors
39. Batteries (MS420)
40. Main Generator/Alternator
    (AR11/D14A)
41. Brake Control Reservoirs

Maximum tractive effort is given as 114,000lb, with a continuous rating of 65,080lb at 14.6mph; this works out as 2,530hp at the rail. The latter is still about 100rhp superior to a Class 56 which has a maximum tractive effort of 61,100lb, thereby showing why substantially greater loads can be handled by Class 59. With a gear ratio of 62:16, Class 59 has a maximum service speed of 60mph and this low gearing is a further influence on the high starting tractive effort. Since the wagons are restricted to 60mph there was no need for anything faster. Locomotive weight is quoted as 124 tonnes; length is 70ft. British AWS, DSD and vigilance have been incorporated. The locomotives can operate in multiple with another class member. GM guarantees a 48hr turnround for spare parts but a number of important components are kept on hand at Merehead. Compare this to lead times of nine months for parts for some BR classes from UK suppliers.

Detailed design and construction took little over 12 months to accomplish at EMD's La Grange works near Chicago. Shipment to the UK was through Southampton on 21-23 January 1986, with movement to Merehead for commissioning on 24 January. On 27 January all four went to Derby for acceptance tests to assess torsional stiffness, brake action, wheel loads, noise levels, cab heating, bogie rotational resistance and ride. Once weighed, two were returned south to permit training of BR personnel, both operating and maintenance, at Westbury and Southall. The DM&EE staff at the Railway Technical Centre continued the testing with the other two

PLAN VIEW

No **1** End

No **2** End

1. Buffers
2. Windscreen Washer System
3. Fire Extinguisher (Both Ends)
4. Electrical Control Cabinet Air Filter
5. Electrical Control Cabinet
6. Filtered Air Compartment Access
7. AWS Equipment
8. Brake Control Valve
9. Hydraulic Parking Brake Unit
10. Vestibule/Corridor
11. Transition Equipment Cabinet
12. WLN Air Compressor
13. Engine Air Filters (Bag Type)
14. Engine Room Bulkhead
15. Engine Access Doors
16. A.C. Cooling Fans (2) - (48" Dia., 9 Bladed "Q" Type)
17. Corridor
18. Door
19. Rear Bulkhead (No. 2 End Only)
20. Fixed Fire Extinguisher System
21. Generator Blower
22. Traction Motor Blower (No. 1 Bogie)
23. Traction Motor Air Duct
24. Inertial Filter Blower
25. Air Brake Rack And Equipment
26. Seat
27. Main Sanding Switch
28. Emergency Brake Valve
29. Handbrake WB & S (Hydraulic)

Below left:
Not all the mileage run by the class is on MGR work. During the coal strike of 1984/85, Class 58 took over the Toton-Ashburys Speedlink and the balancing turn. The latter was invariably a short train, not uncommonly only a single vehicle. On 23 August 1984, No 58010 passes Chinley on its return journey.
A. O. Wynn

Left:
Although designed for all forms of freight, Class 58 has been used almost totally on coal traffic. Around the Birmingham area, though, some mileage has been run on Freightliners. No 47093 had failed in the Birmingham area whilst powering the Coatbridge-Southampton Freightliner on 10 May 1987 and so No 58001, the doyen of the class, provided assistance. The train is approaching Harbury Tunnel, south of Leamington.
Steve Turner

and this included visits to Toton depot, for load bank and noise level tests (in the process the load bank was burned out), and runs to Manton and Cricklewood for ride and braking purposes. The only area where BR requirements were not met was in terms of the ride coefficient, and work continued into 1987 on this point.

Obviously there was considerable interest in seeing how the GM Super Series would translate into haulage capability on BR so some special trials, using rails dressed to give virtually nil adhesion, were staged on 1/2 February on the start out of Merehead. No 59002 was used, initially with 34, 37, 40 and finally 43 102-tonne PTAs; all bar the last loading could be restarted on the 1 in 126 ruling gradient. During the run with the 37 wagons train of 3,774 tonnes, a maximum tractive effort of 114,000lb, equal to 42% adhesion, was measured and this constituted a world record for a Super Series locomotive. A sustained maximum on starting of 111,000lb proved the peak was no isolated figure. A week later trials on Savernake bank, the ruling gradient on the West of England main line, aimed at establishing an ability to restart a maximum load train, but No 59002 failed and so a rerun was arranged for 16 February using No 59001, with No 59004 'dead' inside as reserve, hauling 43 PTAs and two Class 56s at the tail. This 4,639-tonne load was restarted successfully and the following day, 17 February, the locomotives entered service.

Often overlooked are the special instructions governing the operation of these private-owner vehicles on BR. All fuelling and maintenance is FY's responsibility, though the latter is contracted back to BR under a five-year agreement using staff from Bath Road who travel to Merehead. The standard of repair is laid down by BR and the Area Maintenance Engineer, Bristol, decides if a locomotive is fit to run. If a Class 59 fails it will be removed to the nearest refuge to clear the line and then it is FY's responsibility. Conversely, BR may purloin a Class 59 without prior agreement from FY to clear the line, in the event of one of its locomotives failing and the Class 59 is the most expeditious method of so doing. Only BR crews may drive them on BR tracks. It can therefore be seen that the overriding theme is that,

although not BR property, whilst on BR they are totally under Railway control.

A set of new diagrams came into operation on 11 May 1986 to reflect Class 59 utilisation. Maximum service load was 43 PTAs on the run up to Acton, other workings not being so heavy, often due to capacity at termini. This meant 17,470 tonnes of stone could be moved each day. Following a trial run on 31 October when No 59004 took 46 PTAs (4,692 tonnes) on the 00.15 Purfleet service, this became the maximum service load. In consequence a daily tonnage of 19,493 was being moved, representing an 11.5% increase in productivity. Subsequently though, following a Class 59 sticking in section on Warminster bank out of Westbury, it seems that the load limit of the Botley and Eastleigh trains has been cut. Booming demand for aggregates in the Southeast brought the decision by FY in early 1988 to order a fifth example, which was delivered in June 1989. A sample of a week's working for the fleet is set out in Table 1.

Table 1: Class 59 Weekly Operating Cycle

Date (1986)	59001	59002	59003	59004
5/10 6/10	Merehead	Merehead	Merehead	2121 Botley
	a			0600
	d 0015 Purfleet	0425 Acton	0300 Theale	0720 Eastleigh
	a 1510	1300	1115	1600
	d 2011 Botley	1418 Theale	1240 Wootton Bassett	1705 Brentford
7/10	a 0520	2300	2100	0300
	d 0720 Eastleigh	0300 Theale	0015 Purfleet	0425 Acton
	a 1600	1530	1530	1300
	d 2011 Botley	1240 Acton	1705 Brentford	1418 Theale
8/10	a 0520	0020	0300	0300
	d 0720 Botley	0300 Theale	0425 Acton	0015 Purfleet
	a 1600	1115	1300	1530
	d 2011 Botley	1240 Wootton Bassett	1705 Brentford	
9/10	a	2100	0300	
	a 0520			
	d 0720 Eastleigh	0300 Theale	0425 Acton	0015 Purfleet
	a 1600	1115	1300	1530
	d 1705 Brentford	1240 Wootton Bassett	1415 Theale	2011 Botley
10/10	a 0300	2100	2300	0520
	d 0425 Acton	0015 Purfleet	0300 Theale	0720 Eastleigh
	a 1300	1530	1115	1600
	d 1410 Theale		1705 Brentford	Botley
11/10	a 2300			
	a		0300	
	d			0330 Theale
	a			1200

During the period from commissioning to the end of December 1986 a total of 272,829 miles had been accumulated with a total of 19 failures, equal to 14,360 miles per casualty. This is roughly double the Class 56 figure but about on a par with Class 58. As some of the failures represent teething troubles, the figure subsequently has been much higher. To be fair, some of the failures were down to British components and none were, in any event, serious. Some modifications have been incorporated based on initial experience. As delivered, the injectors were all interconnected, so that the failure of one brought a total failure of the locomotive. This has since been altered by fitting individually-sprung injectors (normal practice by British manufacturers but more expensive). During light engine movements it was noticed that, due to the amount of sand dropped automatically if a locomotive was opened up, it would cancel the track circuit and cause the locomotive to disappear from a signalling panel. A modification was therefore fitted to enable the driver to isolate auto sanding during light engine running.

The above problems are minor compared to those encountered with equivalent BR Type 5s. Undoubtedly part of the reason for the success in traffic is due to the quality of maintenance. Whilst all members of the Bath Road artisan staff were encouraged to apply for the 12 positions within the maintenance team who would work on the class, careful selection ensured capable and reliable employees were chosen. Although working without supervision at Merehead, the staff are conscious that any failure can be traced back easily to one person which is not the case in a large depot environment. There is thus both greater pride and care in work and this reflects in performance on the road. In 1986 the LMR launched a Lococare policy to raise staff interest and awareness and the ultimate objective of better maintenance and better availability resulted. It is considered that FY has got a good deal from BR in terms of repair work, something that could probably not be repeated for every major customer. Of course a well-planned design helps make repairs easy, and this also raises staff morale. For example, No 59003 was derailed at Purfleet on 8 December 1987. Stemming from damage caused by movement of plastic rubbing rings in the bogies it became necessary to lift the locomotive. It took just half an hour to disconnect all relevant bogie cabling to facilitate the lift. The same job on a BR locomotive would take several hours.

Traincrews regard the Class 59 as the best prime movers they have ever driven. Indeed, this view is shared just about universally by BR staff who have been involved with them. Such acceptance is vital to the successful operation of any fleet. It had been feared that the rail unions would 'black' them, due to their not being British products. It speaks well of the attitude of the unions, and the work of the BR Employee Relations Department, that this did not happen. Their arrival and performance has served to bring a radical rethink in BR freight train operation and locomotive design concepts. GM designs its locomotives based on the use of poor quality maintenance staff. There is thus no reason why British designs should not be thought out in a similar way but retain the advantage of the high quality of workmanship actually performed at depots. Servicing times could be cut and so locomotive down-time reduced, offering higher productivity. It will only be by raising productivity that Railfreight will achieve the target return on capital and expand its market share and be successful. FY has demonstrated this principle well and, with quarry output of 4 million tons in 1988, placed an order for the fifth Class 59 in March of that year. Lest we run away with excessive praise for the Merehead operation, it must be remembered that FY gets an extremely good deal from BR. If, for example, tyre turning is needed, the Canton wheel lathe is made available during the weekend (in preference to BR machines) to enable Monday-Friday diagramming to be maintained. Such ways of working could never apply on BR as a whole.

Right:
Inevitably, Class 58 has seen use on passenger trains. This has come about in several ways, the haulage of nominally electrically-powered services, diverted off their normal routes, emergency substitution for a failure and specials. The Bootle branch in Liverpool normally only sees passenger traffic on Grand National day. On 27 June 1987 Pathfinder Railtours took the 'Aintree Hurdler' railtour down the branch to the Aintree CLC station; No 58042 was the motive power. *A. O. Wynn*

Left:
It is perhaps not appreciated just how much Class 58 activity now takes place on the ER, with locomotives outstationed at Barrow Hill and Shirebrook. Again, the duties are almost exclusively the movement of MGR coal from pits in Derbyshire and North Nottinghamshire, principally to Trent Valley power stations. A feature of the routes in this area is that they have not been subject to resignalling to any great extent. This gives the contrast of a modern, heavy-haul freight operation, running amid some infrastructure dating from the pre-Grouping era. The driver of No 58037 has just stopped to speak to the signalman in Whitwell's Midland-pattern box, whilst working the 14.36 Thoresby colliery to West Burton power station on 3 November 1988. The former goods shed survives on the left.
Geoff Hurst

CHAPTER 9

Type 5 Freight Performance

Yorkshire Coal

Class 56 was built to handle the increased traffic flows arising from the CEGB's change in fuel policy during the early 1970s in favour of coal. It is therefore worth looking at the performance of an example, hauling coal between pithead and power station. In June 1988 the ER authorities provided footplate facilities to enable the work of a typical turn off Knottingley depot to be studied.

Knottingley provides the motive power for the coal traffic associated with the Aire Valley power stations and associated collieries, together with those in the Doncaster area. Normally there are 18 diagrams each weekday and some Sunday work. During the week commencing 31 May only 10 weekday diagrams were being covered due to colliery holidays. Table 2 shows those appertaining to Drax power station.

A further point was that Ferrybridge power station was closed at the time for major repairs to the rail discharge system. All the turns off Knottingley are booked for a Class 56 hauling a standard rake of 36 HAA hoppers. A trailing load behind the engine of upwards of 1,700 tonnes means that over 1,100 tonnes of coal are being transported, equal to 55 lorries. As can be seen from the table, Drax obtains its supply from a variety of sources and the duty accompanied on 1 June was 7K76, which plied between Selby and Drax over two drivers' shifts. Normally a third shift would have been covered, as can be seen from the full diagram set out here:

Knottingley dep 06.10 light engine
Milford arr 06.23 dep 06.44
Selby arr 06.49 dep 07.54 to Drax arr 08.37 dep 09.34
Selby arr 10.11 dep 11.16 to Knottingley 11.39/11.41 to Drax arr 12.04 dep 12.56
Selby arr 13.33 dep 14.38 to Drax arr 15.21 dep 16.18
Selby arr 16.53 dep 18.00 to Knottingley 18.20/18.22 to

Table 2: Power Station Occupation Week Commencing 31 May 1988 Drax

Trip No	From		Arr	Dep	Empties to	
7K93	2006 MSX	Rossington	0017	0114	MTX	York Yard North
7K86	0006 MTX	York Yard North	0114	0211	MTX	York Yard North
7K87	2252 WTHFO	Goldthorpe	0135	0227	THFSO	Sudforth Lane
7K80	2336 WTHFO	Rossington	0251	0348	THFSO	Milford
7K94	0057 MTX	Frickley	0328	0420	MTX	Milford
7K93	0256 MTX	York Yard North	0404	0501	MTX	Milford
7K82	2336 TO	Rossington	0430	0527	WO	Milford
7K82	0323 THFO	Frickley	0554	0646	THFO	Milford
7K76	0754 MSX	Selby	0837	0934	MSX	Selby
7K80	0730 WTHFO	Goldthorpe	1014	1106	WTHFO	Goldthorpe
7K89	1002 MSX	Selby	1045	1142	MSX	Selby
7K82	0845 MSX	Frickley	1116	1208	MSX	Frickley
7K76	1116 MSX	Selby	1204	1256	MSX	Selby
7K87	0959 WTHFO	Goldthorpe	1243	1335	WTHFO	Goldthorpe
7K93	0824 WTHO	Rossington	1330	1427	WTHO	Sudforth Lane
7K89	1324 MSX	Selby	1407	1459	MSX	Sudforth Lane
7K94	1225 MSX	Frickley	1456	1548	MSX	Frickley
7K76	1438 MSX	Selby	1521	1618	MSX	Milford
7K80	1357 WTHFO	Goldthorpe	1640	1732	WTHFO	Goldthorpe
7K82	1501 MSX	Frickley	1732	1824	MSX	Frickley
7K87	1626 WTHFO	Goldthorpe	1909	2001	WTHFO	Goldthorpe
7K94	1841 MSX	Frickley	2112	2204	MSX	Frickley
7K86	1548 MSX	Rossington	2136	2229	MSX	York Yard North
7K80	2023 WTHFO	Goldthorpe	2246	2338	WTHFO	Doncaster
7K82	2117 TO	Frickley	2348	0040	WO	Doncaster
7K82	2117 WTHO	Frickley	2348	0040	THFO	Frickley
7K82	2117 FO	Frickley	2348	0040	SO	Milford

Drax arr 18.49 dep 19.40
Selby arr 20.17 dep 21.22 to Drax arr 22.05 dep 23.02
Milford arr 23.36 dep 00.02 light engine to Knottingley arr 00.17

The two intermediate calls at Knottingley are for crew changes. As is now the norm on BR fitted freight, DOO applies, which means that normally only the driver travels on the train. Five loaded runs are therefore called for in each daily cycle, meaning that some 5,500 tonnes of coal will be moved by a single locomotive, three drivers and one set of wagons. Fuel and inspection takes place when the machine is on the depot between 00.17 and 06.10.

Train 7FK76 was joined at Knottingley during its first crew change at 11.30. Driver Les Nicholson took charge and Traction Inspector George Sykes was also present. A log of the journey is set out in Table 3.

Table 3: Knottingley-Drax-Selby-Knottingley

Date: 1/6/88
Train: 7K76 Selby-Drax Target
Loco+load: No 56087+36 HAA hoppers

Miles	Location	Actual	Speed (mph)
00.00	Knottingley	00.00	
0.42	Knottingley East Junct	2.17	sigs 42sec
		tsr	20
4.57	Whitley Bridge Junct	12.32	44
7.37	Drax Branch Junct	17.39	20/40 max
			sigs 8min 30sec
11.50	Drax power station	44.30	8min late
00.00		00.00	14min late
4.13	Drax Branch Junct	10.09	49 max/25*
5.47	Hensall	12.15	49
11.08	Knottingley East Junct	—	sigs 30sec
		pause	
11.50	Knottingley	21.43	sigs 15sec
12.49	Ferrybridge Power Station Junct	24.58	25
		tsr	25
14.60	Burton Salmon Junct	28.39	sigs 2min
16.37	Milford Junct	35.59	30
		sigs	
17.84	Gascoigne Wood Junct	39.43	25
—	Selby Complex	40.31	17min late
—		00.00	6min late
00.00	Gascoigne Wood Junct	1.23	25
1.47	Milford Junct	5.16	30
		tsr	20
3.24	Burton Salmon Junct	9.46	30
		sigs	5
5.35	Ferrybridge Power Station Junct	16.13	28
6.59	Knottingley	20.33	

Departing at 11.28, 13min early, the journey to Drax power station passed without incident. It was surprising how easily No 56087 coped with its load of 36 full HAAs; there was very limited use of full power, it just was not needed. The load limit for a Class 56 over this route is 45 HAAs but the ER keeps its wagons in standard 36 rake sets, this being the longest that can be accepted at all Yorkshire and North East pits. On starting Driver Nicholson generally used 2,000A to get the train moving. Full power was not applied until about 15mph had been attained. Inspector Sykes explained that drivers are instructed to keep the needle in the continuous rating band on the cab ammeter at 2,700A. Turning off the former Lancashire and Yorkshire Railway's route to Goole at Hensall Junction, one of the very few remaining sections of the old Hull & Barnsley Railway (H&B) provides access to Drax; this bit of line was relaid for the purpose, having been previously closed.

Turning into the power station off the H&B, which continues as a short spur to hold replacement wagons, should a defective vehicle have to be removed from a set, the train crosses a weighbridge. For proper weighing, speed must not exceed 15mph. Traversing the power station circuit it was necessary to wait some distance short of the discharge point to allow a preceding train to unload. Although there are three discharge roads only two were in use on the day in question. An exit road is provided which allows trains to avoid going through the unloading point, should this be necessary for any reason. Eventually unloading of 7K76 commenced at 12.12, 8min late. The road used for discharge was the one which feeds direct into the power station's furnace and so the rate of discharge is governed by the demand for coal at that precise moment. As well over 1,000 tonnes of coal are burnt every hour this does not normally delay a train. The other two discharge roads send their coal to the large stockpile, which can then be fed into the furnace as needed. A second train was also being unloaded at the same time as 7K76 and, once this had cleared, another entered the discharge point straight away. During discharge the locomotive is operated in slow-speed mode at 0.5mph. This is selected by the driver, who applies a partly opened power controller, and the control system then maintains the preset speed automatically.

Unloading, carried out automatically, actually took 68min and, coupled with the wait for a road into the discharge area, Drax was left 14min late. These days freight train punctuality is not a matter left to chance. Freight contracts have been lost due to poor performance and some trains carry a penalty clause for late delivery. Obviously, for services such as those to the Aire Valley power stations, reliability on BR's part is very important. Plant breakdowns at either loading or unloading can cause havoc with programmed working, but that is not the railway's responsibility. Hence reliable motive power is essential and in this respect Class 56

Above right:
Merehead is the home base of the Class 59 fleet, although they are actually allocated to Headquarters. This line-up of Nos 59001-5 was taken at Merehead on 25 June 1989. With a silver and blue livery, there is no difficulty distinguishing them from a BR diesel. In the background is the building in which maintenance is carried out. *C. R. Holland*

Right:
The fifth Class 59 locomotive arrived in the UK at Felixstowe on 4 June 1989. Named *Kenneth J. Painter* **and looking resplendent in FY livery, No 59005 is seen here on display at Merehead on 25 June 1989.** *C. R. Holland*

Left:
The haulage trials were carried out on the WR West of England main line between Westbury and Savernake. They involved the haulage of maximum load trains, with restarts on the steepest climb on the route. On the second of the trials on 16 February 1986 Nos 59001/4 stand at Woodborough.
J. Chalcraft

acquits itself satisfactorily. Before departure the wagons were inspected for signs of hot axleboxes and doors which had not been closed properly by the equipment. Defective vehicles can then be removed before leaving the power station complex.

Whereas on the loaded journey the train was limited to 45mph for brake force reasons, it now ran as a Class 6 train, 6K76, and could travel at up to 55mph. A facility is provided at Drax for drivers to be relieved at the entrance to the power station to enable them to take a personal needs break whilst their train is unloaded. To cover the unloading a Knottingley driver is based there and on the return journey one was picked up and transported back to the depot, having completed his shift; this accounts for the pause in the log just prior to Knottingley station. Pulling away from this station on dry rails some slipping took place. Another bout of slipping occurred later in the journey and both seemed to be due to No 56087 being able to develop a tractive effort higher than could be sustained even under apparently good rail conditions. Driver Nicholson allowed the electronic control system to arrest the slipping and reapply power, the response time by the system being impressively quick.

A short interruption for signals at Burton Salmon allowed a York-Sheffield DMU to cross in front and then 6K76 made its way down past Gascoigne Wood Junction to gain access to the concentration point for coal mined at the British Coal Selby complex. Before proceeding down to the overhead loading terminal a train preparer was collected. The journey time from Drax had been just over 40min.

Unfortunately when the terminal was designed, ground water problems restricted its height, with the result that insufficient clearance was available under the loading bays to permit a locomotive to pass through. A time-consuming shunt is therefore needed and hence part of the need for a train preparer. First the empty train draws down the site. Then the locomotive is uncoupled and runs round, drawing the wagons forward towards Gascoigne Wood to enable it to clear the points which allow a change of road on to one leading to a loading point. Now the train sets back until the driver's side cab window is exactly in line with a marker pole which ensures that the leading vehicle is correctly positioned for loading whilst there is no danger of the driver reversing too far and knocking the rear cab against the overhead equipment.

Loading of each wagon is automatic and takes about 11min for the entire train, roughly 100 tonnes of coal/min. If a wagon is known to be defective then the computer controlling the loading can be programmed to omit that vehicle without any manual input. The usual throughput at Selby is 25 trains per day, the coal coming from five mines which are all linked; eventually, as coal production rises, the output from Selby will grow. Just beyond Hensall Junction, where the Drax branch leaves the Goole line, a spur used to enable movements from the Goole direction to gain northbound access to the East Coast main line. Although abandoned many years ago, consideration is being given to relaying it, as this would shorten considerably the journey time between Drax and Selby. It would still entail trains being propelled empty under the loading hoppers but would at least remove the need for a run round. During the day, however, pathing along the East Coast main line would be virtually impossible and the cost of the connections would be very costly just for use at night. A further examination of the train takes place prior to departure.

As the loading process had taken only 54min, 7K76, now carrying 1,110 tonnes of coal, was able to depart only 6min behind schedule. Once more, the journey back to Knottingley proved uneventful and at 14.58 the train was halted at the crew change point to allow the footplate passengers to alight. No 56087 had done everything that was required to move its train between pithead and power station. The good rail conditions did not allow a proper test of the adhesion capabilities but the impression gained was that this was not a problem. Riding was good, a cup of coffee was not slopped, something that would certainly have happened on a Class 47. Noise levels were unobtrusive in both cabs, even under full power. It was also remarkable how little the maximum capabilities of the Type 5 were called upon, bearing out the generally accepted figure of full power being used for about 3% of total operating time. Driver Nicholson had no specific complaints about the apologies.

The main source of
failures was due to overheating, caused by loss of
coolant, and this has been referred to in Chapter 4. All in
all, this was a very respectable and workmanlike
performance.

Driver Nicholson took No 56087 through Drax for a
second time and then returned the empty wagons to
Milford Sidings, before running light back to Knottingley.
Normally he would have made a second trip into Selby,
instead of leaving the wagons at Milford, and before
beeing relieved on his way back to Drax. The relieving
driver would then have completed the journey to Drax
and made another return trip to Selby and back before
finally depositing the wagons at Milford and going on the
depot. Whilst mileages are not high, this sort of
operation is certainly intensive and also offers a good
testimony to the design. Bearing in mind the limited
demand for full power, it is interesting to consider the
possibility of a Class 37/7 substituting for a Type 5, as
starting tractive effort would be identical.

Mendip Stone

It is understood that the most arduous work assigned to
Class 56 is that associated with the movement of stone
out of the quarries in Somerset. No 56001, when fitted
with new Napier Mk 3 turbochargers, was reallocated to
the WR for trials in the Westbury area. The movement of
stone from its quarry at Merehead was the reason why
Foster Yeoman bought a fleet of General Motors Class
59s. Looking at how both these types perform on the
road therefore makes an interesting comparison. During
1986 Mr Martin Beckett was permitted to make two
footplate journeys on the FY Merehead-Theale service,
firstly when Class 56 was still rostered for the work, then
later in the year when the American imports had arrived.
Table 4 sets out the Westbury to Theale part of the
journey.
The two runs are not absolutely comparable, for
No 56045 was hauling four-wheeled stock whilst
No 59003 had a rake composed primarily of bogie
hoppers. At the time the load limit for a Class 56 was
2,300 tonnes; this has since been raised to 2,500 tonnes.

Table 4: Westbury-Theale

Run 1: 07.00 Merehead-Theale 24/1/86 No 56045+43 vehicles, 2,287 tons full
Run 2: 14.18 Merehead-Theale 4/7/86 No 59003+30 vehicles, 2,660 tons full

Distance miles			Run 1 min.sec mph		Run 2 min.sec mph	
00.00	Westbury station	dep	0.00	—	0.00	—
00.97	Heywood Road Junction		3.53	32	3.20	30
08.56	mp 87 (Lavington)		14.16	51	13.14	54
14.56	mp 81 (Patney)		23.41	39	21.35	40
16.56	mp 79 (Woodborough)	arr	28.37	—	24.16	46 pass
20.23	Pewsey		8.26	43	28.47	52
22.56	mp 73		11.51	45	31.35	50½
25.56	mp 70 (Savernake)		16.17	39	35.23	43
27.56	mp 68 (Crofton)		18.48	55	37.39	60
29.13	Bedwyn		20.28	57/54	39.10	62/60
34.02	Hungerford		26.16	47	44.10	58
37.06	Kintbury		29.36	57	47.14	60
42.46	Newbury		35.30	57	53.26	tsr/35*
43.17	Newbury Racecourse		36.12	55	54.29	37
45.99	Thatcham		39.14	57	58.06	56
48.82	Midgham		42.13	58	60.58	62
50.77	Aldermaston		44.17	57/tsr 20*	62.51	62
53.90	Theale Sidings	arr	54.02	—	70.26	—
Net running time from Westbury			76min		69min	

Run 1: Driver K. Butt (Westbury); Traction Inspector R. Allaway
Run 2: Driver J. Jones (Westbury); Traction Inspector R. Allaway   * Speed restriction

Unfortunately no figures for the respective rolling
resistance of either type are available. No 56045 also had
to contend with an adverse wind, though the Class 59
had a heavier load. Good rail conditions prevailed on
both days so there was no opportunity to see the GM
Super Series wheelcreep system in operation.
Leaving Westbury the overall tendency is uphill until
Savernake is passed. There is an initial sharp pull out of
the yard and up to Heywood Road Junction, where the
Westbury avoiding line is joined. A similar driving style
was used for No 56045 as to No 56087, namely about
2,000-2,200A to get the train away, with full power at 10
to 15mph. By comparison, No 59003 was put into Notch 5
out of 8 to start, giving 5,600A, quickly moved to full after
about 30sec, with over 6,000A being delivered to the
traction motors. With these motors being connected in
all-parallel, as compared to series-parallel for Class 56,
the currents taken are twice as great. In other words,
6,000A on an all-parallel machine is the same as 3,000A
for a series-parallel one. The difference in starting effort
showed itself in the times taken to pass Heywood Road
Junction, the relative speeds also reflecting the
superiority of the Class 59.

Right:
The Merehead-Purfleet service is usually loaded to 46 bogie wagons and this makes it the heaviest train on BR. After splitting the train in Acton yard, the Class 59 proceeds to Purfleet via the North London line. No 59003 *Yeoman Highlander* passes Canonbury on the North London line on 14 May 1988. *Brian Morrison*

Right:
Class 59 ventures on to Southern metals via Salisbury, en route to Botley and Eastleigh stone terminals. In this view, taken on 9 June 1986, No 59004 *Yeoman Challenger* brings empty PGA wagons from Eastleigh over Quarry Junction on the approach to Merehead. *C. R. Holland*

Until reaching Lavington the road is virtually level, except for a short 1 in 100 past Edington. Along this bit of railway both locomotives accelerated their trains well but No 59003 had reached 54mph by now, against only 51mph for No 56045; the time gained by the former had reached a minute. During this section the Class 56 had taken its field divert at the predicted 48mph. Climbing to Patney, at a ruling gradient of 1 in 222, No 56045 fell away to 34mph but had recovered to 39mph before power was shut off for the train to be looped at Woodborough so that an IC125 could pass. Naturally, with its flying start, the Class 59 had the better of things up Savernake Bank, which concludes at 1 in 156, but even allowing for No 56045 having to assault the climb from a lower initial speed, it would not, on previous experience, have matched the time and speed of the nominally similarly rated Class 59. Until this point the Class 59 had been driven at full power since leaving Westbury. With the 4,600-tonne Purfleet service a single Class 59 clears Savernake at about 14mph.

From Savernake it would be possible to coast down to Theale. To avoid bunching of the train, with the risk of breaking a coupling due to snatching when power is reapplied, it is customary to use light power during the descent to keep the couplings taut. Even allowing for its faster run whilst virtually coasting, the net time calculated by Mr Beckett still favours No 59003 by a fair margin, giving it a decided advantage over its British counterpart.

On the return leg No 56045 had to be driven with bursts of full power on the climb up the Kennet Valley to Savernake. Although the gradients are not quite as steep as those in the up direction, with a maximum of 1 in 173, nevertheless the 60mph maximum permitted to the train was not held. It might be considered that the wind which had been adverse on the outward run would now assist, but in fact this was not the case. The high-sided PGA hoppers, when empty, generate internal eddy currents which add markedly to their drag factor. Indeed a modification has been considered in the form of baffles inside the vehicle to break up these flows. With a clear road, though, No 56045 was able to average 49mph. No 59003 was not favoured with such a clear run. The

Table 5: Theale-Westbury

Run 1: 24/1/86 No 56045+43 vehicles, 675 tons gross
Run 2: 4/7/86 No 59003+30 vehicles, 570 tons gross

Distance miles		Run 1 min.sec	mph	Run 2 min.sec	mph
00.00	Theale Sidings West (mp 42) dep	0.00	—	dep 0.00	—
02.79	Aldermaston	7.34	46	5.07	53
04.74	Midgham	10.04	54	7.06	62/60
07.57	Thatcham	13.14	56	9.52	60
10.39	Newbury Racecourse	16.21	58	12.41	52/sigs
11.10	Newbury	17.03	60	arr 15.13	—
16.50	Kintbury	22.51	57/58	7.14	60
19.54	Hungerford	26.05	58	10.16	60
24.43	Bedwyn	31.19	56	15.01	63
26.00	mp 68 (Crofton)	33.08	52	16.30	62
28.00	mp 70 (Savernake)	35.31	49	18.27	61
33.33	Pewsey	41.14	59	23.43	63
37.00	mp 79 (Woodborough)	45.15	58	27.14	55/sigs 3min
45.00	mp 87 (Lavington)	53.54	53	44.06	61
52.59	Heywood Road Junction	63.28	25*	51.44	25*
53.20	Signal W296 arr	65.03	—	—	—
53.56	Westbury station	—	—	arr 54.46	—

Run 1: Driver T. Pearce (Westbury); Traction Inspector R. Allaway
Run 2: Driver J. Jones (Westbury); Traction Inspector R. Allaway
* Speed restriction

train was put inside at Newbury to allow a Class 47-hauled passenger train to pass, whilst later in the journey there was a signal stop due to a suspected track circuit failure.

Both drivers expressed a liking for their motive power. At the time of the run with No 56045 the Class 59s had only just made their way from Southampton Docks to Merehead, having arrived at Wesbury whilst the run was in fact taking place. Apart from failures due to overheating, there was no particular adverse remark against Class 56. Ride and noise levels were both considered as good. With Class 59 the ride was also rated equal to Class 56, whilst the bigger silencer makes the machine about 10% quieter than a Class 56, though it is not as quiet as a Class 58.

Class 58 in Winter

By kind permission of the LMR, footplate facilities were made available for 7V65, the 13.50 Three Spires-Didcot power station MGR. The date of the run was 26 February 1986 at a time when the weather was very cold but otherwise fine. Temperatures, except where in direct sunlight, were well below freezing. At this time it must be admitted that the class was going through a bad spell for failures and on the previous day 7V65 had suffered two Class 58 failures before even clearing Coventry, whilst the rostered unit on the day of the journey had failed on the first part of the diagram, causing No 58021 to be substituted after an earlier round trip to Didcot. The latter was stabled at Coventry Goods in the short holding siding just on the Birmingham side of the station. Normally the locomotive would have been brought from Bescot by a train crew off that depot. A further complication was that the Proof House diversions were disrupting normal operations in the Birmingham area in any event and so the crew were later arriving than booked.

Table 6: Coventry-Banbury

Train: 7V65, 13.50 Three Spires-Didcot power station
Formation: 58021+30 HAA wagons, 485 tonnes tare, 1,471 tonnes gross
Weather: Fine, dry, frosty, wind from southeast
Drivers: Jellings (to Coventry) and Thorpe; Traction Inspector Harland
Date: 26/2/86

Miles			Actual times	Speed (mph)	Remarks
00.00	Three Spires	dep	00.00	27 max	
03.04	Coventry Goods		10.37/34.07		Brakes dragging
03.56	Coventry		36.40		
07.69	Kenilworth Loop N End		46.26	45	
12.32	Milverton		54.57	20*	Sigs
			56.05/57.29		Sig stop
12.96	Leamington N Junction		59.04		
13.18	Leamington Spa		60.00	5*	Sigs
13.51	mp 105¾		62.28		
			tsr	25*	
14.76	mp 104½		65.44		
16.76	Fosse Road mp 102½		69.04	40	
18.61	Harbury Tunnel N End		71.38	45	Eased at 70min 53sec
19.31	Southam Road		72.35	44	
20.10	Greaves Sidings		73.39	45	
24.28	Fenny Compton Loop		82.04/91.04		
24.51	mp 94¾			20	Slipping in cutting
				42 max	
33.08	Banbury Loop	arr	113.08	—	

* Speed restriction

Mention of train crew indicates more than one person and whilst technically DOO applies, there being no guard, for this turn a secondman was rostered with the driver. Those concerned were Driver Jellings and Assistant Driver Thorpe (who had just passed his Class 58 driver's course); Traction Inspector Harland of Rugby was also present. On checking the locomotive it was noted that the coolant level was low and so, rather than risk a failure on the road, a trip light to Saltley was needed; this was complicated by the Proof House

diversions and was made via Nuneaton and Water Orton. An advantage of this visit was the opportunity to ride a Class 58 at close to its design speed of 80mph and certainly there were no grounds for complaint in this respect. Equally, although full power was not used, the acceleration of a 3,300hp machine running light was phenomenal. The cab environment was generally good but the large expanse of glass did mean that it cooled quickly in the prevailing temperatures although with the cab heater on it quickly became very warm. The seating was comfortable and visibility excellent; there was ample room for the two additional passengers. The only adverse aspect was the vibration of parts of the cab bulkhead and door when under power, presumably due to loose fittings, something one would not expect in so new a locomotive.

At Three Spires a load of 30 HAA wagons grossing 1,471 tonnes was collected though it took half an hour to obtain brake pressure and departure was some 3hr late. This perhaps serves to illustrate how a freight train can become late as, unlike passenger trains, there may not be a substitute unit to hand in the event of a failure, plus there is no trainload of passengers to consider. Running down the line towards Coventry the train air brake pressure was dropping and at Coventry Goods it was deemed essential to stop, although under clear signals, rather than risk the brakes coming on fully whilst negotiating the busy junction through Coventry station. Although pressure was quickly recovered it was some time before the train was signalled to proceed.

Despite a trailing load of little under 1,500 tonnes, once on the line to Leamington acceleration to the permitted 45mph for the train was rapid and most of the way only about half power was being used. Undoubtedly the interesting part of the journey was the climb to Southam Road which is the steepest bank on the route, with gradients of 1 in 172. Once clear of Leamington station full power was used but again 45mph was attained quite effortlessly and there was a distinct lack of the sensation that such a heavy load was being pulled. Apart from the rattles mentioned previously and the cab heater there was virtually no other noise, as there should not be since the design of silencer makes Class 58 an exceptionally quiet runner. Being so late it was inevitable that the train would get sidetracked to let faster traffic overtake and this happened at Fenny Compton where a 20min wait was needed so that a labouring Class 31 could struggle by on fertilizer vehicles, its speed little above what 7V65 would have been doing.

On restarting, Assistant Driver Thorpe used the normal procedure employed during the run of partly opening the power controller until the train was running at between 10mph and 15mph before applying full power. Once in the cutting to the south of the site of Fenny Compton station the rails became icy due to the lack of sunlight during the day and No 58021 slipped repeatedly. Although there was a slight easing of the controller the locomotive was left on virtually full power, with the load regulator automatically reducing power to the wheels and applying sand without intervention by the driver. Speed did not drop noticeably and once out of the cutting the prevailing adhesion returned to normal. Approaching Banbury the train was again signalled into the loop and here regrettably the footplate run was curtailed to permit the passengers to get home that night, as by now it was approaching 19.00. The crew were booked to be relieved at Didcot by a Reading driver who would take the train through the power station before a fresh Bescot crew would return the empties to the LMR.

Even though the part of the ride during which a train was actually being hauled was not long, it was possible to assess the ability of No 58021 in carrying out its work. There was no difficulty in starting a train of 1,500 tonnes, equally the load regulator was fully up to controlling wheelslip without driver intervention, returning normal power when conditions allowed. With some 2,650hp available at the rail it was not surprising that 45mph could be attained and held regardless of gradient. A 2,070-tonne load limit applies to Class 58 over this route. The ride quality and cab environment were good and the crew had no specific complaints about the class.

In order to provide an example of a full day's diagram for a Class 58 engaged on the long hauls to Didcot, Figure 9 gives the full picture. Originating from Saltley, the driver takes the locomotive light engine to Three Spires colliery

Figure 9: Class 58 Diagram

Train Working	Arr.	Dep.	WTT No.	Days Run
No. 22 (Amended)				
Worked by 21 MO				
21 MSX				
CLASS 58 (SSC/AB)				
Saltley LIP		07 59	LD	SX
Three Spires Jn	09 05	09 34	7V44* AIR	SX
Didcot PS	12 16	13 30	6M38* AIR	SX
Three Spires Jn	15 14	15 30	LD	SX
Saltley LIP	16 28			
Saltley LIP		18 49	LD	SX
Three Spires Jn	19 50	20 24	7V90* AIR	SX
Didcot PS	22 31	23 55	6M30* AIR	SX
Coventry Goods	01 25	01 45	LD	MX
Saltley LIP	02 27 FUEL			
Works 23 MSX				
23 SO				

sidings on the Coventry-Nuneaton line. Running time to Didcot is 2¾hr, with just over an hour for unloading. After bringing back the empty rake of HAAs and leaving them at Three Spires, the locomotive is returned to Saltley for stabling before taking up the second half of the turn. This involves a second return trip from Three Spires to Didcot, finishing up again at Saltley, where refuelling and daily inspection will be carried out. A total daily mileage of 368.4 is involved, of which 102.6 miles are run light engine. Some 2,000 tons of coal will be moved in the process.

Passenger Work

There has never been any regular diagramming of the current Type 5 classes for passenger work. Frequent use

Right:
**On the occasion of the
footplate run described in
this chapter, here
No 56087 is seen
emerging from the
discharge point at Drax.
Another MGR is also
unloading.**
David N. Clough

Left:
**Due to late running, it
was not possible to
secure any pictures of the
footplate run with
No 58021 en route.
On 11 September 1985,
No 58015 is caught by the
camera passing Radley,
heading for Didcot.**
Colin Grafham

has been made of them east of Birmingham during Sunday engineering diversions to take nominally electrically-hauled trains over non-electrified routes. Appearances during emergencies have seen some interesting feats of haulage, as have already been noted, but full performance logs are elusive. Railtours have provided an opportunity to gain haulage and examine performance potential. Unfortunately, though, the high power and relatively low top speed often means the true abilities of the motive power cannot be fully displayed.

Table 7: Carlisle-Preston

Date: 22/8/87
Train: Swindon-Newcastle charter
Loco+load: No 56016+11 Mk 2ds
Train weight (tons): 367/395

Miles	Location	Actual	Speeds (mph)
00.00	Carlisle	00.00	
4.91	Wreay	7.36	65½
7.35	Southwaite	9.37	78½
13.10	Plumpton	13.50	84½
17.89	Penrith	17.25	75½/77
22.07	Clifton	20.39	78½
29.40	Shap	26.21	76½min/77½
31.35	Shap Summit	27.52	79½/91
37.00	Tebay	31.47	87/77
41.10	Low Gill	34.42	78
42.97	Grayrigg	36.07	77
44.85	Lambrigg	37.32	84/88
49.96	Oxenholme	44.10	77
55.56	Milnthorpe	45.16	83
62.85	Carnforth	50.27	91
69.10	Lancaster	56.234	sigs 33/86
		delays	
90.10	Preston	88.15	

A Pathfinder railtour to the north during August 1987 included a southbound run over Shap and a late start out of Carlisle gave an incentive for time recovery. Table 7 sets out the details. No 56016 was not fully opened out until Upperby Junction, but very rapid acceleration was then achieved. It is possible there was an easing back after Southwaite as the train was nearly up to the 80mph top speed mark, despite the 1 in 228 climb. Only on the level stretch past Plumpton was the 80mph mark actually crossed. Taking the slow start and top speed into account, it was very good work to pass Penrith in under 17½min. The assault of Shap from the north is mainly on a 1 in 125, with a 75mph speed limit round the curves past Thrimby Grange. Rain, which had begun to fall after Wreay, persisted though seemed to cause no problem as

No 56016 was driven flat out uphill. The load and grade combined to bring speed into line with prevailing limits, giving a 77.6mph average from Eden Valley Junction to Shap. Such an effort required 3,060hp at the rail, about 400hp more than the performance curve for Class 56 predicts. As the load was double-checked on arrival at Preston the accuracy of the data is beyond doubt, signifying a gross engine output of well over 3,500bhp.

Kestrel

Although not specifically relevant to this chapter, it has been possible to demonstrate the work of HS4000 *Kestrel* during its short period of activity on East Coast passenger duties. The two logs set out in Table 8 have been supplied by the Railway Performance Society. The left-hand columns describe a run with *Kestrel's* usual load of eight coaches, whilst the other columns show the work of the locomotive on a 12-coach service.

Table 8: King's Cross-Darlington

Date: 20/10/69
Train: 07.55 King's Cross-Newcastle
Loco+HS4000 *Kestrel*+8
Train weight (tons): 276/290

25/10/69
11.30 ex-Doncaster
HS4000 *Kestrel*+12
394/430

Miles	Location	Actual	Speeds	Actual	Speeds
00.00	King's Cross	00.00			
2.51	Finsbury Park	4.43	60/84		
12.75	Potters Bar	12.56	78		
		sigs	20		
26.75	Langley Junct	25.40	92		
32.00	Hitchin	30.10			
		tsr	29/103		
58.84	Huntingdon	48.00	92		
		tsr	30		
63.50	Abbots Ripton	52.28	78/91		
76.36	Peterborough	62.57	20		
84.80	Tallington	71.04	98/103		
97.09	Corby Glen	78.27	99/103		
100.09	Stoke	80.15	99/103		
105.50	Grantham	83.58	67/102		
120.14	Newark	93.17	80/84		
138.59	Retford	107.17	82		
		tsr	31		
		tsr	27		
155.96	Doncaster	124.18	63/94		
174.25	Selby	138.44	52/42/93		
188.31	York	151.30	25	00.00	
189.95	Skelton Junct	154.21	53	3.06	56
193.81	Beningbrough	157.37	91/102	6.21	81/95
198.86	Tollerton	160.15	100/98	9.11	93
204.34	Pilmoor	164.05	101	13.04	100* 102
210.56	Thirsk	167.43	103	16.43	101/103
218.31	Northallerton	172.42	85/69	21.19	100
227.31	Eryholme	180.02	84	26.50	80
		sigs	15sec		
232.41	Darlington	186.56		31.21	

CHAPTER 10
Class 60 and The Future

General Motors had been developing its Super Series high adhesion system, known as wheelcreep, since 1972; it was first applied to a locomotive in 1978. The latter year was when the BRB decided to run with the BREL-inspired low cost freight design which turned into Class 58. Hence at the time that Class 58 was being conceived it was no match for what GM could offer in terms of high adhesion; put less charitably, it was out of date in that respect whilst still on the drawing board. It was not until the FY-bought, GM-built Class 59s proved their superiority over any existing BR type in Merehead quarry and on the Berks & Hants line that the railway hierarchy seems to have woken up to just what they should be specifying in terms of a Type 5 freight design.

To be fair, during 1985 Brush had commenced work on developing a scheme to improve the utilisation of adhesion, which takes advantage of the already-good characteristics of dc traction motors. In this new development the field coils are excited and controlled separately, rather than by using the armature current, as with series-wound motors. The abbreviation SEPEX was coined and this method of control steepens the motor's characteristic so that the torque of a motor driving a slipping axle drops dramatically to facilitate the arrest of the slip. A groundspeed radar was fitted to provide accurate measurement of track speed. The trials were carried out on the Old Dalby test track and in Sutton colliery during 1986 using Class 47, No 47543. This demonstrated that significantly higher adhesion levels were possible with the new equipment. Following on from this came the equipping of No 58050 for SEPEX operation, as mentioned in Chapter 6.

Whilst the engineering world was applying state-of-the-art electronics to give the best possible performance from a diesel-electric locomotive, the government was redefining the financial performance of BR, including the Railfreight Sector. By the end of the decade the latter would have to be yielding a 5% return on capital employed and so it was becoming essential to get the maximum tractive effort per pound of money spent. Stemming from this came the realisation that the best rate of return could be achieved by deploying high availability, high reliability, high adhesion Type 5s to operate heavy-haul coal and mineral traffic; Speedlink and Freightliners neither offered the same potential nor demanded the same pulling power. Lessons learned with Class 59 pointed the way and, indeed, there were many who would gladly have accepted a fleet of these machines for wide use in the two sub-Sectors.

On 10 August 1987 the BRB issued tenders and detailed specification documents for 100 of its next generation of Type 5 freight engines. Requirements included a 3,300bhp rating, top speed of 60mph and the ability to start a 2,800-tonne train on a 1.0% gradient; also taken into account were life cycle costs, including repair and fuel costs, and a track record for the equipment to be installed. Just exactly which companies were invited to tender is not clear, but, aside from those who did, it is known that General Electric of America declined the offer. Documents were received from three, a consortium between GEC and GM (which offered a design based on Class 59), Metro-Cammell and Brush. Metro-Cammell's submission seems to have been by way of offering various configurations of other manufacturers' equipment, for the company is merely an assembler and does not produce either diesel engines or electrical machines itself.

In June 1988 the Secretary of State for Transport announced that Brush had been awarded the contract and an outline of their proposal is shown in Figure 10. A Mirrlees-Blackstone eight-cylinder, four-stroke diesel, Model 8MB275T, rated at 3,100bhp at 1,000rpm has been chosen. One of the factors in favour of the Brush proposal was the fuel economy offered by this diesel,

Right:
The best route on which to assess the work of Class 59 is the Berks & Hants and this is why Martin Beckett's journey was made between Westbury and Theale. No 59001 *Yeoman Endeavour* **is seen at Lock on 19 March 1987 with the 09.30 Theale-Merehead.** *Brian Morrison*

Left:
Class 60 No 60002
***Capability Brown* is seen**
in Brush's Falcon Works
at Loughborough on
12 August 1989.
Barry J. Nicolle

**Figure 10: Class 60
General Arrangement**

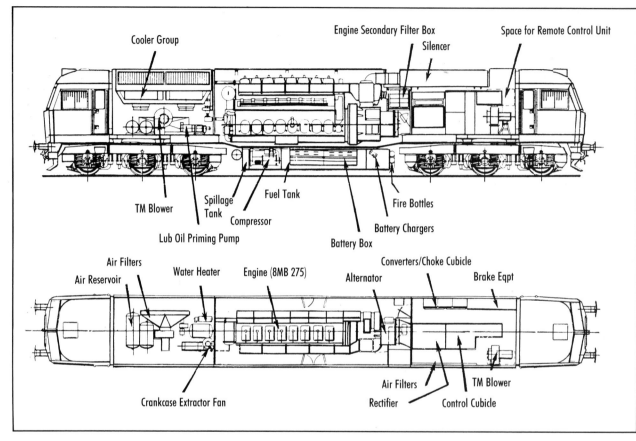

when compared to its GM counterpart used in Class 59. It also had the advantage of having passed the BR type-testing programme. It is a tall but slim unit, which created a height problem, counterbalanced by affording good engine room access. A large silencer means that the UIC 100db noise limit is adhered to. A six-cylinder version of this engine has been in service in four Class 37/9s for over two years.

Coupled to this is a Brush main alternator but, unlike those fitted to the previous British Type 5s, this has slip-rings and is not brushless. It is a BA 1006A model, rated at 2,055kVA, 375V, 3,160A at 1,000rpm. An eight-pole, dual wound auxiliary alternator is attached to the end of the alternator shaft which supplies the three-phase auxiliaries. This is model No BA 702A. A separate six-phase winding is used to excite the main and auxiliary alternators and the SEPEX traction motors. It is also the source of ac for other systems within the locomotive.

Located at No 1 end is the cooler group, which has two radiator fans. These are driven by Brush three-phase induction motors and their operation is determined by the temperature of the cooling system so that none, one or two fans operate. The radiator panels are protected against dirt by a coarse grille and fine mesh cover. At the same end there is a traction motor blower, compressed air reservoirs, the engine lubricating oil priming pump and crankcase extractor fan. No 2 end compartment has a second traction motor blower, the control cubicle, rectifiers and brake frame. Primary air filtration is by swirl-type inertia filters, mounted in the bodyside at this end. The filtered air passes through this compartment for cooling the equipment and is drawn through a duct by the self-ventilating main alternator, also to provide cooling. It then passes into the engine room for cooling and clearance of fumes. To maintain a positive air flow there are vents in the roof and at No 1 end of the engine room. The compartment at No 1 end has its own air supply for the blower motors, with its own inertia filter.

Whereas Class 58 and Class 59 both feature a strength underframe, Brush has opted instead for monocoque body construction for Class 60. The main reason seems to be to save weight, about 5 tonnes, but internal access does not suffer unduly. Four removable roof panels allow access to the engine, whilst two double doors on either side of the locomotive mean maintenance staff can enter the engine room without having to pass through the cabs. The slim profile of the diesel is an advantage. Two compressors and the fuel tank are underslung from the underframe, with the battery boxes attached to the tank. Internal layout of the cabs follows the principles developed for Class 58.

Bogie design is of the fabricated frame type and has aimed at minimising weight transfer during starting, coupled with low maintenance. It is derived from that used in Classes 56, 58 and 89 and the Co-Co wheel arrangement sees the six four-pole traction motors connected in all-parallel. These motors are Brush TM 2161A four-stroke units rated continuously at 300kW, 462V, 700A at 472rpm. Gearing is for 60mph and a maximum tractive effort of 112,400lb compares with 60,700lb for a conventional Class 58.

No form of wheelcreep control is included. It is contended that wheelcreep does not cope well with coal dust slurry contamination on the rails found in colliery yards. As might be expected, though, state-of-the-art microprocessor technology is used within the control scheme. By substituting a slip-ring alternator for the previous brushless machines used in Classes 56 and 58, the aim has been to quicken response time to varying control demands. With SEPEX traction motors offering an inherent antislip characteristic, the control system is less concerned with detecting and arresting an axle which is running away. Instead, the objective is to monitor motors not developing their full tractive effort.

The system is continually assessing whether or not the various outputs are causing the overall tractive effort to rise or fall. This means that an effective system of control is available not only to provide high adhesion at low speed but also across the full speed range of the locomotive.

Construction of the body has been subcontracted to Procor at Horbury, West Yorkshire, with the shell, painted internally and externally, delivered to Falcon works for fitting out. The alternators are supplied from Brush to Mirrlees at Stockport, where they are fitted to the diesel and tested statically, before return to Brush for installation. Bogie manufacture is on site at Loughborough. The first body arrived for fitting out early in 1989 and No 60001 was delivered to BR in early July. It was, at the time of writing, being put through a full series of commissioning trials before entering service in 1990. The rate of production will be geared up to enable the full order to be in service by 1992.

Even as the Class 60 contract was being let plans began to emerge for a bigger version in the shape of Class 65. It is understood that this would be of around 4,000bhp and be designed for 75mph work. Whether this will come to pass cannot be judged at present; other similar projects, notably the smaller Class 38, have been shelved or abandoned in the past. On a more certain front, in June 1989 ARC announced that it had placed an order with GM for four Class 59s. These will be based at Westbury for stone traffic in the area, and will be painted in the company's livery.

Appendix 1 Table of Dimensions

Type	HS4000 *Kestrel* Co-Co	Class 56 Co-Co	Class 58 Co-Co	Class 59 Co-Co	Class 60 Co-Co
Overall length	66ft 6in	63ft 6in	63ft 4in	70ft	70ft
Overall width	9ft 2in	9ft 2in	8ft 10in	8ft 8in	—
Overall height	12ft 11in	12ft 9in	13ft	12ft 10in	13ft
Bogie wheelbase	14ft 11in	13ft 5½in	13ft 8in	13ft 6in	13ft 7in
Wheel diameter	3ft 7in	3ft 8in	3ft 9in	3ft 6in	3ft 8in
Minimum curve negotiable	4 chains	3.5 chains	4 chains	4 chains	4 chains
Weight	131 tonnes	126 tonnes	129 tonnes	126 tonnes	126 tonnes
Maximum service speed	110mph	80mph	80mph	60mph	60mph
Fuel tank capacity	1,000gal	1,120gal	985gal	1,000gal	1,000gal
Maximum engine output	3,946bhp at 1,100rpm	3,250bhp at 900rpm	3,300bhp at 1,000rpm	3,300bhp at 904rpm	3,100bhp at 1,000rpm
Maximum tractive effort	70,000lb	60,600lb	61,800lb	113,750lb	112,400lb
Continuous tractive effort	41,200lb at 27.5mph	54,000lb at 17mph	53,950lb at 17.5mph	65,080lb at 14mph	75,500lb
Power at rail	3,020rhp	2,450rhp	2,520rhp	2,535rhp	—
Gear ratio	19:60	16:63	16:63	15:62	19.97

Note: In compiling the above table numerous variations in dimensions between sources have been revealed. The most reliable source has therefore been used.

Appendix 2 Dates to Traffic and Names

Class 56

Locomotives	Date to traffic	Name and date of naming
56001	28/2/77	*Whatley* 29/10/87
56002	28/2/77	
56003	28/2/77	
56004	28/2/77	
56005	14/3/77	
56006	25/2/77	
56007	13/4/77	
56008	13/4/77	
56009	27/5/77	
56010	28/7/77	
56011	29/6/77	
56012	18/4/77	*Maltby Colliery* 22/6/89
56013	1/8/77	
56014	28/3/77	
56015	21/3/77	
56016	27/5/77	
56017	13/5/77	
56018	23/8/77	
56019	13/5/77	
56020	20/5/77	
56021	17/6/77	
56022	24/5/77	
56023	11/7/77	
56024	15/6/77	
56025	5/7/77	
56026	15/7/77	
56027	19/9/77	
56028	14/9/77	*West Burton Power Station*
56029	12/9/77	
56030	21/10/77	*Eggborough Power Station* 2/9/89
56031	24/5/77	*Merehead* 16/9/83
56032	19/7/77	*Sir De Morgannwg/ County of South Glamorgan* 14/10/83
56033	2/8/77	
56034	25/8/77	*Castell Ogwr/Ogmore Castle* 5/6/85
56035	13/10/77	*Taff Merthyr* 9/11/81 (now removed)
56036	17/8/78	
56037	20/1/78	*Richard Trevithick* 23/7/81

56038	19/2/78	Western Mail 2/6/81
56039	7/2/78	
56040	15/2/78	Oystermouth 25/3/83
56041	15/2/78	
56042	14/5/79	
56043	31/3/78	
56044	14/5/78	
56045	1/6/78	
56046	18/7/78	
56047	28/7/78	
56048	19/9/78	
56049	11/10/78	
56050	25/10/78	
56051	4/11/78	
56052	6/12/78	
56053	29/12/78	Sir Morgannwg Ganol/ County of Mid Glamorgan 17/3/86
56054	26/1/79	
56055	1/2/79	
56056	12/3/79	
56057	27/3/79	
56058	29/4/79	
56059	16/5/79	
56060	9/6/79	
56061	9/8/79	
56062	29/8/79	Mountsorrel 21/3/89
56063	6/9/79	Bardon Hill
56064	17/9/79	
56065	17/10/79	
56066	11/12/79	
56067	11/12/79	
56068	11/12/79	
56069	11/12/79	
56070	21/12/79	
56071	21/12/79	
56072	7/1/80	
56073	29/2/80	
56074	23/3/80	Kellingley Colliery 14/6/82
56075	6/4/80	West Yorkshire Enterprise 9/7/85
56076	14/4/80	Blyth Power 8/9/82 (now removed)
56077	18/5/80	
56078	25/5/80	
56079	22/6/80	
56080	13/7/80	
56081	24/8/80	
56082	24/8/80	
56083	7/9/80	
56084	26/10/80	
56085	21/1/81	
56086	7/12/80	
56087	21/12/80	
56088	25/1/81	
56089	25/1/81	
56090	8/3/81	
56091	21/6/81	Castle Donnington 18/6/89
56092	21/6/81	
56093	28/6/81	
56094	9/8/81	
56095	16/8/81	Harworth Colliery 29/10/87
56096	13/9/81	
56097	4/10/81	
56098	18/10/81	
56099	8/11/81	Fiddler's Ferry Power Station
56100	15/11/81	
56101	21/12/81	
56102	20/12/81	
56103	27/12/81	
56104	21/2/82	
56105	28/3/82	
56106	25/4/82	
56107	16/5/82	
56108	20/6/82	
56109	15/8/82	
56110	3/10/82	
56111	24/10/82	
56112	21/11/82	
56113	12/12/82	
56114	23/1/83	
56115	30/1/83	
56116	13/3/83	
56117	13/3/83	
56118	17/4/83	
56119	15/5/83	
56120	29/5/83	
56121	19/6/83	
56122	3/7/83	Wilton — Coalpower 14/4/88
56123	31/7/83	Drax Power Station 11/5/88
56124	25/9/83	Blue Circle Cement 24/10/83
56125	20/10/83	
56126	15/11/83	
56127	13/12/83	
56128	18/12/83	
56129	8/1/84	
56130	1/4/84	
56131	29/4/84	Ellington Colliery 20/8/87
56132	10/6/84	Fina Energy 1/10/86
56133	29/7/84	Crewe Locomotive Works 2/6/84
56134	9/9/84	Blyth Power
56135	4/11/84	Port of Tyne Authority 29/10/85

Class 58

Locomotives	Date to traffic	Name and date of naming
58001	6/2/84	
58002	6/2/84	Daw Mill Colliery 17/3/89
58003	6/2/84	

Locomotive	Date	Name
58004	6/2/84	
58005	6/2/84	
58006	6/2/84	
58007	6/2/84	
58008	6/2/84	
58009	6/2/84	
58010	13/2/84	
58011	11/3/84	
58012	11/3/84	
58013	11/3/84	
58014	5/4/84	Didcot Power Station 11/6/88
58015	18/9/84	
58016	5/10/84	
58017	24/10/84	
58018	30/10/84	High Marnham Power Station 21/5/88
58019	23/1/85	
58020	18/3/85	Doncaster Works BRE 7/11/84 (later to Doncaster Works)
58021	17/12/84	
58022	7/1/85	
58023	7/2/85	
58024	7/2/85	
58025	5/3/85	
58026	29/3/85	
58027	19/4/85	
58028	19/4/85	
58029	19/4/85	
58030	21/6/85	
58031	3/10/85	
58032	23/9/85	
58033	16/10/85	
58034	11/11/85	Bassetlaw 12/12/85
58035	2/1/86	
58036	13/2/86	
58037	11/3/86	
58038	11/3/86	
58039	13/3/86	Rugeley Power Station 13/9/86
58040	18/3/86	Cottam Power Station 20/9/86
58041	27/3/86	Ratcliffe Power Station 6/9/86
58042	13/6/86	Ironbridge Power Station 27/9/86
58043	10/7/86	
58044	8/9/86	
58045	1/10/86	
58046	23/10/86	
58047	11/11/86	
58048	8/12/86	
58049	22/12/86	Littleton Colliery 14/3/87
58050	8/3/88	Toton Traction Depot 3/5/87

Class 59

Locomotives	Date to traffic	Name and date of naming
59001	21/1/86	Yeoman Endeavour 28/6/86
59002	21/1/86	Yeoman Enterprise 28/6/86
59003	21/1/86	Yeoman Highlander 28/6/86
59004	21/1/86	Yeoman Challenger 28/6/86
59005	25/6/89	Kenneth J. Painter

Class 60

At the time of writing, only six Class 60 locomotives had received names, although it had been announced by Railfreight that all but two of the current order for 100 locomotives would be named. Names currently allocated are shown below:

60001	Steadfast
60002	Capability Brown
60003	Christopher Wren
60004	Lochnager
60005	Skiddaw
60006	Great Gable

Prototypes

Locomotives	Date to traffic	Name and date of naming
47901	17/10/64	Initially numbered D1628 Renumbered 47046 1/73 Renumbered 47601 12/75 Renumbered 47901 11/79
HS4000	14/5/68	Kestrel withdrawn 3/71